The War on Terror

Second Edition

POINT / COUNTERPOINT

The War on Terror
Second Edition

Paul Ruschmann, J.D.

SERIES CONSULTING EDITOR
Alan Marzilli, M.A., J.D.

CHELSEA HOUSE
PUBLISHERS
An imprint of Infobase Publishing

The War on Terror, Second Edition

Copyright © 2008 by Infobase Publishing

Chelsea House
An imprint of Infobase Publishing
132 West 31st Street
New York NY 10001

Library of Congress Cataloging-in-Publication Data

Ruschmann, Paul.
 The war on terror / Paul Ruschmann.—2nd ed.
    p. cm.—(Point/counterpoint)
 Includes bibliographical references and index.
 ISBN 978-0-7910-9834-9 (hardcover)
 1. Terrorism—United States. I. Title. II. Series.

 KF9430.R87 2008
 363.3250973—dc22   2008016982

Chelsea House books are available at special discounts when purchased in bulk quantities for businesses, associations, institutions, or sales promotions. Please call our Special Sales Department in New York at (212) 967-8800 or (800) 322-8755.

You can find Chelsea House on the World Wide Web at
http://www.chelseahouse.com

Series design by Keith Trego
Cover design by Keith Trego and Jooyoung An

Printed in the United States of America

Bang NMSG 10 9 8 7 6 5 4 3 2 1

This book is printed on acid-free paper.

All links and Web addresses were checked and verified to be correct at the time of publication. Because of the dynamic nature of the Web, some addresses and links may have changed since publication and may no longer be valid.

Alan Marzilli, M.A., J.D.
Birmingham, Alabama

The POINT-COUNTERPOINT series offers the reader a greater understanding of some of the most controversial issues in contemporary American society—issues such as capital punishment, immigration, gay rights, and gun control. We have looked for the most contemporary issues and have included topics—such as the controversies surrounding "blogging"—that we could not have imagined when the series began.

In each volume, the author has selected an issue of particular importance and set out some of the key arguments on both sides of the issue. Why study both sides of the debate? Maybe you have yet to make up your mind on an issue, and the arguments presented in the book will help you to form an opinion. More likely, however, you will already have an opinion on many of the issues covered by the series. There is always the chance that you will change your opinion after reading the arguments for the other side. But even if you are firmly committed to an issue—for example, school prayer or animal rights—reading both sides of the argument will help you to become a more effective advocate for your cause. By gaining an understanding of opposing arguments, you can develop answers to those arguments.

Perhaps more importantly, listening to the other side sometimes helps you see your opponent's arguments in a more human way. For example, Sister Helen Prejean, one of the nation's most visible opponents of capital punishment, has been deeply affected by her interactions with the families of murder victims. By seeing the families' grief and pain, she understands much better why people support the death penalty, and she is able to carry out her advocacy with a greater sensitivity to the needs and beliefs of death penalty supporters.

The books in the series include numerous features that help the reader to gain a greater understanding of the issues. Real-life examples illustrate the human side of the issues. Each chapter also includes excerpts from relevant laws, court cases, and other material, which provide a better foundation for understanding the arguments. The volumes contain citations to relevant sources of law and information, and an appendix guides the reader through the basics of legal research, both on the Internet and in the library. Today, through free Web sites, it is easy to access legal documents, and these books might give you ideas for your own research.

Studying the issues covered by the Point-Counterpoint series is more than an academic activity. The issues described in the book affect all of us as citizens. They are the issues that today's leaders debate and tomorrow's leaders will decide. While all of the issues covered in the Point-Counterpoint series are controversial today, and will remain so for the foreseeable future, it is entirely possible that the reader might one day play a central role in resolving the debate. Today it might seem that some debates—such as capital punishment and abortion—will never be resolved.

However, our nation's history is full of debates that seemed as though they never would be resolved, and many of the issues are now well settled—at least on the surface. In the nineteenth century, abolitionists met with widespread resistance to their efforts to end slavery. Ultimately, the controversy threatened the union, leading to the Civil War between the northern and southern states. Today, while a public debate over the merits of slavery would be unthinkable, racism persists in many aspects of society.

Similarly, today nobody questions women's right to vote. Yet at the beginning of the twentieth century, suffragists fought public battles for women's voting rights, and it was not until the passage of the Nineteenth Amendment in 1920 that the legal right of women to vote was established nationwide.

What makes an issue controversial? Often, controversies arise when most people agree that there is a problem, but people disagree about the best way to solve the problem. There is little argument that poverty is a major problem in the United States, especially in inner cities and rural areas. Yet, people disagree vehemently about the best way to address the problem. To some, the answer is social programs, such as welfare, food stamps, and public housing. However, many argue that such subsidies encourage dependence on government benefits while unfairly penalizing those who work and pay taxes, and that the real solution is to require people to support themselves.

American society is in a constant state of change, and sometimes modern practices clash with what many consider to be "traditional values," which are often rooted in conservative political views or religious beliefs. Many blame high crime rates, and problems such as poverty, illiteracy, and drug use on the breakdown of the traditional family structure of a married mother and father raising their children. Since the "sexual revolution" of the 1960s and 1970s, sparked in part by the widespread availability of the birth control pill, marriage rates have declined, and the number of children born outside of marriage has increased. The sexual revolution led to controversies over birth control, sex education, and other issues, most prominently abortion. Similarly, the gay rights movement has been challenged as a threat to traditional values. While many gay men and lesbians want to have the same right to marry and raise families as heterosexuals, many politicians and others have challenged gay marriage and adoption as a threat to American society.

Sometimes, new technology raises issues that we have never faced before, and society disagrees about the best solution. Are people free to swap music online, or does this violate the copyright laws that protect songwriters and musicians' ownership of the music that they create? Should scientists use "genetic engineering" to create new crops that are resistant to disease and pests and produce more food, or is it too risky to use a laboratory to create plants that nature never intended? Modern medicine has continued to increase the average lifespan—which is now 77 years, up from under 50 years at the beginning of the twentieth century—but many people are now choosing to die in comfort rather than living with painful ailments in their later years. For doctors, this presents an ethical dilemma: should they allow their patients to die? Should they assist patients in ending their own lives painlessly?

Perhaps the most controversial issues are those that implicate a Constitutional right. The Bill of Rights—the first 10 Amendments to the U.S. Constitution—spell out some of the most fundamental rights that distinguish our democracy from other nations with fewer freedoms. However, the sparsely-worded document is open to interpretation, with each side saying that the Constitution is on their side. The Bill of Rights was meant to protect individual liberties; however, the needs of some individuals clash with society's needs. Thus, the Constitution often serves as a battleground between individuals and government officials seeking to protect society in some way. The First Amendment's guarantee of "freedom of speech" leads to some very difficult questions. Some forms of expression—such as burning an American flag—lead to public outrage, but are protected by the First Amendment. Other types of expression that most people find objectionable—such as child pornography—are not protected by the Constitution. The question is not only where to draw the line, but whether drawing lines around constitutional rights threatens our liberty.

The Bill of Rights raises many other questions about individual rights and societal "good." Is a prayer before a high school football game an "establishment of religion" prohibited by the First Amendment? Does the Second Amendment's promise of "the right to bear arms" include concealed handguns? Does stopping and frisking someone standing on a known drug corner constitute "unreasonable search and seizure" in violation of the Fourth Amendment? Although the U.S. Supreme Court has the ultimate authority in interpreting the U.S. Constitution, their answers do not always satisfy the public. When a group of nine people—sometimes by a five-to-four vote—makes a decision that affects hundreds of millions of others, public outcry can be expected. For example, the Supreme Court's 1973 ruling in *Roe v. Wade* that abortion is protected by the Constitution did little to quell the debate over abortion.

Whatever the root of the controversy, the books in the Point-Counterpoint series seek to explain to the reader both the origins of the debate, the current state of the law, and the arguments on either side of the debate. Our hope in creating this series is that the reader will be better informed about the issues facing not only our politicians, but all of our nation's citizens, and become more actively involved in resolving these debates, as voters, concerned citizens, journalists, or maybe even elected officials.

September 11, Terrorism, and War

O n September 10, 2001, Americans' greatest concern was the economy: unemployment was rising, the stock market was slumping, and a recession seemed possible. The possibility of a massive terrorist attack was far from their minds. Daniel Benjamin and Steven Simon, who served on the National Security Council under President Bill Clinton, observed, "[M]ost Americans, if asked, would have likely said that their nation had never been more secure. More than a decade after the end of the Cold War, it had become a truism that the world had not seen such a dominant power since ancient Rome."[1]

The Threat of Terrorism

National security experts, however, were concerned that terrorists were about to attack Americans on their own soil. In 1999, the United States Commission on National Security foresaw the possibility of terrorist attacks involving mass casualties and warned, "Americans will become increasingly less secure, *and much less secure than they believe themselves to be.*"[2]

A new and deadly terrorist threat first appeared in this country in 1993, when a powerful truck bomb exploded underneath the World Trade Center in New York City. After the Trade Center bombing, there were increasingly deadly attacks against Americans overseas, as well as terrorist conspiracies to kill Americans at home.

Authorities linked many of the worst incidents to a worldwide organization known as al Qaeda, which means "the base." (*Note*: There is no universally accepted way to translate Arabic words, such as *al Qaeda*, into English. As a result, multiple different spellings of these words appear in English-language publications.) Al Qaeda is led by Osama bin Laden, a wealthy Saudi businessman who had embraced a fundamentalist strain of the Islamic faith. Expelled from Saudi Arabia and later from the Sudan, bin Laden and his followers moved to Afghanistan, where they operated terrorist training camps under the protection of that country's ruling Taliban regime.

Bin Laden made no secret of his intentions. In February 1998, he and five other men issued a *fatwa*, or religious edict, in an Arabic-language paper published in London. As the 9/11 Commission explained: "Claiming that America had declared war against God and his messenger, they [bin Laden and his associates] called for the murder of any American, anywhere on earth, as the 'individual duty of every Muslim who can do it in any country in which it is possible to do it.'"[3]

Three months later, bin Laden told an ABC-TV reporter that he drew no distinction between those in the military and non-combatants. He said:

> We believe that the worst thieves in the world today and
> the worst terrorists are the Americans. Nothing could stop
> you except perhaps retaliation in kind. We do not have to

Above, members of the FBI's counterterrorism division visit a mosque in Brooklyn, New York, shortly after the London terrorist attacks in 2005. Osama bin Laden called upon Muslims everywhere to take action against Westerners, but most Muslims in the United States do not adhere to bin Laden's ideology.

differentiate between military and civilian. As far as we are concerned, they are all targets.[4]

On September 11, 2001, his followers made good on that threat. Terrorists hijacked passenger jets and flew them into the World Trade Center and the Pentagon, killing nearly 3,000 people. Hundreds of thousands witnessed the attacks in person, and billions more around the world saw them on television.

The nation reacted to the attacks with a mixture of grief and outrage. The Bush administration called them an "act of war" and moved quickly to find and punish the terrorists. On September 18, Congress passed the Authorization for the Use of Military Force (AUMF) resolution[5], which authorized the president to use

Some Recent Acts of Terrorism

May 1978: A package bomb sent to Northwestern University injures a campus police officer in the first attack by "Unabomber" Theodore Kaczynski, a violent opponent of technology. Over the following 16 years, his homemade bombs kill 3 people and injure at least 26 others. Kaczynski is arrested in 1996 and later sentenced to life in prison.

April 18, 1983: A Muslim extremist drives a truck filled with explosives into the U.S. embassy in Beirut, Lebanon, killing 63 people, including 17 Americans. The Reagan administration blames the Muslim guerrilla group Hezbollah for the bombing and alleges that Iran and Syria provided support to the bombers.

October 23, 1983: A truck bomb explodes outside a U.S. Marine barracks in Beirut, killing 241 people. Soon afterward, the United States ends its peacekeeping operations in Lebanon. In May 2003, a U.S. federal judge finds that Hezbollah was responsible for the bombing, with funding and approval from high officials in Iran's government.

August–September 1984: In a local election campaign, members of the Rajneesh cult in Oregon contaminate local restaurants with salmonella bacteria in order to make their opponents too sick to vote. About 750 people become seriously ill in the nation's worst incidence of food terrorism.

April 5, 1986: A terrorist bomb kills 3 and injures 229, many of them American service personnel, at a Berlin disco. President Reagan blames Libyan leader Muammar Qaddafi for the bombing.

December 21, 1988: A bomb placed on Pan Am Flight 103 explodes over Lockerbie, Scotland, killing 259 people aboard the plane and 11 on the ground. Evidence found at the crash scene links Libyan intelligence agents to the bombing. Libya eventually turns over the suspected terrorists, who are tried under Scottish law, and the country later agrees to pay $2.7 billion to the victims' families.

February 26, 1993: Islamic fundamentalists detonate a bomb underneath the World Trade Center. Four men are tried and found guilty of the bombing in 1994. The alleged mastermind, Ramzi Yousef, is later tried and convicted for planning the bombing, as is Omar Abdel Rahman.

April 14, 1993: Kuwait's security service uncovers a plot by Iraqi agents to kill President George H.W. Bush with a truck bomb. On June 27, the United States retaliates by launching a cruise missile attack on Iraqi Intelligence Service headquarters in Baghdad.

(continues)

(continued)

March 20, 1995: Aum Shinrikyo, a doomsday religious cult, releases nerve gas in 6 Tokyo subway stations, killing 12 people and sending about 5,000 to hospitals.

April 19, 1995: A truck bomb explodes outside the Alfred P. Murrah Federal Building in Oklahoma City, killing 168 people. Timothy McVeigh and Terry Nichols, army veterans with ties to extreme right-wing causes, are charged. McVeigh is sentenced to death, Nichols to life in prison.

June 25, 1996: A truck bomb explodes outside American military apartments in al-Khobar, Saudi Arabia, killing 19 and injuring hundreds. Federal prosecutors later allege that Hezbollah terrorists were responsible and that Iranian officials lent them support.

July 27, 1996: A pipe bomb planted at the Olympic Games in Atlanta kills 1 person and injures 111. In November 2000, federal authorities charge Eric Robert Rudolph, a Christian extremist, for that bombing. He is finally apprehended in June 2003.

August 7, 1998: Simultaneous truck bombs explode outside the American embassies in Kenya and Tanzania, killing 225 and injuring more than 4,000. Federal prosecutors accuse Osama bin Laden of orchestrating the bombings and file charges against a number of his followers. In May 2001, four men are convicted for their role in the bombings. Their trial reveals details about al Qaeda's organization and business dealings.

"all necessary and appropriate force" against those responsible for the attacks. This legislation was also intended as a means to prevent further attacks. Two days later, the president told a joint session of Congress and the American people that the nation was at war with terrorists. He warned the rest of the world, "Either you are with us, or you are with the terrorists. From this day forward, any nation that continues to harbor or support terrorism will be regarded by the United States as a hostile regime."[6]

The president specifically demanded that the Taliban hand over al Qaeda's leaders and close down the terrorist training camps. When his ultimatum was refused, a U.S.-led military

October 12, 2000: A bomb carried on a small boat explodes near the destroyer USS *Cole* at Aden, Yemen, killing 17, injuring 39, and severely damaging the *Cole*. The 9/11 Commission later concludes that the attack on the *Cole* was "a full-fledged al Qaeda operation, supervised directly by bin Laden."

September 11, 2001: Hijackers fly passenger jets into the World Trade Center and the Pentagon, killing nearly 3,000 people. On October 7, the United States leads an invasion that overthrows Afghanistan's ruling Taliban regime; kills or captures thousands of enemy fighters, including many of al Qaeda's leaders; and dismantles al Qaeda's training camps.

October 12, 2002: Truck bombs destroy two nightclubs in Bali, Indonesia, killing 202 and injuring 200. The main suspects are members of Jemaah Islamiyah, an Islamic extremist group with ties to al Qaeda.

March 11, 2004: A series of bombs at a train station in Madrid, Spain, kills 191 people and injures more than 1,400. Authorities determine that the attacks were carried out by Islamic extremists who were locally organized, but that the terrorists had connections to outside fundamentalist groups and might have been overseen by a "supreme leader."

July 7, 2005: Four suicide bombers kill themselves and 52 passengers in the London Underground and on a double-decker bus. British authorities are still unsure who masterminded the attack, but believe that the plot went beyond the four suicide bombers. Two of the four had been in contact with people in Pakistan who had links to al Qaeda.

force working with anti-Taliban Afghans known as the Northern Alliance launched an invasion that drove the Taliban out of the country's major cities. Coalition forces killed or captured thousands of Taliban fighters, as well as many of al Qaeda's leaders. Bin Laden himself was never found, and he is believed to have survived the attack. His al Qaeda organization was weakened by the invasion, but it continues to function.

"A Different Kind of War"

President George W. Bush told the country that the fight against terrorism would be a "different kind of war":

This war will not be like the war against Iraq a decade ago, with a decisive liberation of territory and a swift conclusion. It will not look like the air war above Kosovo two years ago, where no ground troops were used and not a single American was lost in combat.... Americans should not expect one battle, but a lengthy campaign, unlike any other we have ever seen. It may include dramatic strikes, visible on TV, and covert operations, secret even in success.[7]

The September 11 attacks have been compared to the bombing of Pearl Harbor, the event that propelled the United States into World War II. However, the September 11 hijackers were a different enemy than the Japanese pilots who bombed Pearl Harbor. They lived among Americans while plotting to kill them, were not wearing military uniforms on the day of the attacks, and were fighting on behalf of a cause rather than a country.

The invasion of Afghanistan illustrated the difference between traditional conflicts and the fight against terrorism. One major target was the Taliban, which few countries recognized as Afghanistan's legitimate government. The Afghan people were for the most part innocent bystanders, and it was hard for anti-Taliban fighters to distinguish friends from enemies.

Balancing Liberty and Security

After September 11, the nation's leaders concluded that national security deserved a higher priority, even at the expense of individual liberty. President Bush assumed many of the broad powers of earlier wartime presidents. One of his first actions was to authorize military trials of non-U.S. citizens who were responsible for the attacks themselves or who engaged in terrorist activity in general. Meanwhile, federal agents scoured the country looking for people with possible links to terrorists. They asked thousands of men from Arab and Muslim countries why they were in the United States and what they knew about terrorist activity. They also strictly enforced immigration laws and seized the assets of charities and other organizations with suspected ties to terrorist groups.

The Bush administration also asked for new legal tools to fight terrorism. Congress quickly responded by passing the USA PATRIOT Act (Patriot Act)[8], a sweeping law that created new terror-related crimes, gave intelligence agencies and the police broader powers to monitor suspected terrorist activity, and made it easier for government agencies to share information. The Patriot Act was heavily criticized at first, but much of the controversy subsided over time; Congress renewed it in 2006 with relatively few changes to its key provisions.

Redefining Foreign Policy

President Bush announced that the United States would adopt a strategy for national security that focused on preventing future acts of terrorism. In his 2002 State of the Union address, he defined the new threat that the nation faced. He singled out Iran, Iraq, and North Korea as an "axis of evil." The president considered those countries the most dangerous because they had both the motive and the means to provide terrorists with weapons of mass destruction (WMDs)—chemical, biological, or nuclear devices that can kill thousands, even millions, of people. Faced with such a threat, the president concluded that a national security policy developed during the Cold War was no longer appropriate: "Deterrence—the promise of massive retaliation against nations—means nothing against shadowy terrorist networks with no nation or citizens to defend. Containment is not possible when unbalanced dictators with weapons of mass destruction can deliver those weapons on missiles or secretly provide them to terrorist allies."[9]

In his 2002 National Security Strategy document, the president also made it clear that the United States would not ask other countries' permission before taking action: "While the United States will constantly strive to enlist the support of the international community, we will not hesitate to act alone, if necessary, to exercise our right of self-defense by acting pre-emptively against such terrorists, to prevent them from doing harm against our people and our country."[10]

The Bush Doctrine was applied first against Iraq. For months, President Bush warned the rest of the world that Iraqi dictator Saddam Hussein had WMDs. When the United Nations refused to take swift action to disarm Hussein, Bush formed a "coalition of the willing" (a group of countries willing to take military action) that forcibly removed him from power. Even though the Iraq war has lasted longer and has resulted in more American casualties than the administration anticipated, the president insists that leaving Hussein in power would have led to even worse consequences. His 2006 National Security Strategy document quotes the findings of a team of weapons inspectors who went into Iraq after the invasion:

> Virtually no senior Iraqi believed that Saddam had forsaken WMD forever. Evidence suggests that, as resources became available and the constraints of sanctions decayed, there was a direct expansion of activity that would have the effect of supporting future WMD reconstitution.[11]

What Is Terrorism?

Terrorism is as old as history itself, and it has often been associated with religious conflict. Three words in our language—"thug," "zealot," and "assassin"—originally referred to members of ancient Hindu, Jewish, and Muslim extremist sects. Terrorism has been more common during some periods of history than others, and the tactics used by terrorists have changed over the years.

The use of the word "terror" to describe this phenomenon was coined during the French Revolution, when the governing regime used its emergency powers to arrest and execute thousands of accused traitors. France's Reign of Terror was an example of *state terrorism,* violence committed by a government against its own citizens. State terrorism was prevalent in much of

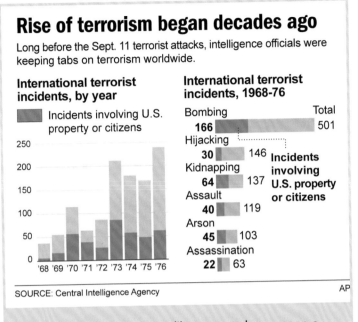

Rise of terrorism began decades ago

Long before the Sept. 11 terrorist attacks, intelligence officials were keeping tabs on terrorism worldwide.

International terrorist incidents, by year

- Incidents involving U.S. property or citizens

250
200
150
100
50
0

'68 '69 '70 '71 '72 '73 '74 '75 '76

International terrorist incidents, 1968-76

		Total
Bombing	**166**	501
Hijacking	**30**	146
Kidnapping	**64**	137
Assault	**40**	119
Arson	**45**	103
Assassination	**22**	63

Incidents involving U.S. property or citizens

SOURCE: Central Intelligence Agency   AP

Although terrorism may seem like a recent phenomenon, a rise in terrorist attacks began decades before September 11, as demonstrated in the chart above.

the world during the mid twentieth century. Regimes of both the left (Mao Zedong's China and Joseph Stalin's Soviet Union) and the right (Adolf Hitler's Nazi Germany) subjected millions of people, including their own citizens, to arbitrary arrests, torture, mass imprisonment, and even wholesale slaughter. Nowadays, terrorism is associated with violence committed by individuals, directed at public officials or civilians, and aimed at forcing the government to change its policies.

Many historians trace modern-day terrorism to the radical anarchists of the nineteenth century. Anarchism, a movement against established authority, began in tsarist Russia. Violent anarchists tried to assassinate high government officials in an effort to publicize their cause. Some also hoped that their actions would provoke a government crackdown that might cause a revolution. The movement spread to other countries, including the United States. In 1901, an anarchist by the name of Leon Czolgosz assassinated President William McKinley.

Terrorism was part of some countries' struggles for independence during the twentieth century; one example is the Republic of Ireland. During World War II, some resistance fighters in occupied countries resorted to terrorism against the Nazi occupiers. And during the 1960s, left-wing guerrillas fought pro-American regimes in Latin America. Some terrorist movements were supported by foreign states. For example, the Soviet Union and Iran lent support to Middle Eastern terrorist groups fighting Israel.

The current wave of terrorism began in the 1980s. It tends to be motivated by religious or ethnic hatred, often uses suicide bombers, and, as the September 11 attacks demonstrated, can kill large numbers of civilians. Most people associate terrorism with the Middle East, but terrorist movements operate in other parts of the world, as well. Non–Middle Eastern terrorist groups include the Shining Path in Peru and the Liberation Tigers of Tamil in Sri Lanka. There also are homegrown terrorists in the United States, in addition to cells linked to movements based overseas. To date, the most notorious domestic terrorists were right-wing extremists Timothy McVeigh and Terry Nichols, who were responsible for the 1994 Oklahoma City bombing.

The war on terror is less black and white than conflicts such as World War II. It is often said, "One man's terrorist is another man's freedom fighter." For example, many believe that the people of Chechnya, a region in southern Russia, are legitimately fighting for independence. The Russian government, however, treats them as terrorists. The same is true of Palestinians rebelling against Israeli rule in the West Bank and Gaza. There is also a problem of defining what terrorism is. Modern terrorist networks raise money in a number of ways, including posing as charities soliciting donations and engaging in crimes such as cigarette smuggling. As a result, it is sometimes hard to draw a

Americans Who Fight with the Enemy:
Hamdi v. Rumsfeld

An unusual facet of the fight against terror is the handful of American citizens who fought alongside the enemy. Lawsuits challenging their captivity raised the question of whether Americans enjoy greater legal protection than non-citizen enemy fighters. One such individual was Yaser Hamdi. He was captured in Afghanistan by members of the Northern Alliance and turned over to the U.S. military. When it was learned that Hamdi was an American citizen, he was transferred to a military prison inside the United States.

Hamdi's father filed a habeas corpus petition on his son's behalf. In the district court, the government argued that Hamdi's detention was lawful if it could produce "some evidence"—a very low standard—that he was an enemy combatant. The government's evidence was a declaration by a Defense Department official that Hamdi had affiliated with a Taliban military unit, stayed with it after September 11, 2001, and was captured on an Afghan battlefield with an assault rifle in his possession.

The U.S. Court of Appeals for the Fourth Circuit reversed the district court's decision. It criticized the lower court for not giving greater deference to the president in deciding who should be detained as an enemy combatant in a time of war. Nevertheless, the appeals court rejected the government's argument that courts had no business reviewing the president's decision to declare an individual an enemy combatant. Hamdi appealed the decision to the United States Supreme Court, which, in *Hamdi v. Rumsfeld*, 542 U.S. 507 (2004), ruled in his favor.

There were multiple opinions, but eight of the nine justices concluded that the government could not hold Hamdi indefinitely without a hearing. Justice Sandra Day O'Connor's plurality opinion attracted four votes, one short of a majority. Justice O'Connor found it unnecessary to decide whether the president had inherent power as commander in chief of the armed forces to hold enemy prisoners—a question that remains unanswered—because he had been authorized to do so by the September 2001 Authorization for the Use of Military Force (AUMF) resolution. That resolution, as O'Connor read it, authorized the detention of the "limited category" of captured Taliban and al Qaeda fighters.

Even though courts would not question the government's initial decision to detain an enemy fighter, Justice O'Connor declared that an American citizen

(continues)

(continued)
who disputed his enemy combatant status was entitled to some measure of due process. Without offering details, she stated that due process entitled a citizen to know why he was declared an enemy combatant, and to be given a fair opportunity to rebut the government's evidence.

Justice David Souter, joined by Justice Ruth Bader Ginsburg, contended that the AUMF did not authorize Hamdi's indefinite detention, and that another federal statute specifically prohibited it. They added that the government's treatment of captured enemy fighters violated the Third Geneva Convention, which required that a fighter's status be determined by a "competent tribunal," after which he would either be charged with war crimes, detained as a prisoner of war, or set free.

Justice Antonin Scalia argued that the government could not detain an American citizen as an enemy combatant: It must either bring criminal charges against him or set him free. If the president thought it necessary to indefinitely detain Americans, he would have to ask Congress to pass a law suspending habeas corpus. Justice Scalia also pointed out that the American constitutional tradition has been to bring criminal charges, such as treason, against U.S. citizens who waged war against their own country.

Only Justice Clarence Thomas supported the government's position. In his view, courts had no authority to second-guess the lawfulness of Hamdi's detention, even if the decision to detain him was mistaken. He called the issue of Hamdi's status "of a kind for which the Judiciary has neither aptitude, facilities, nor responsibility," especially because a lawsuit could require the government to divulge classified information. Justice Thomas added that the logic of Justice O'Connor's opinion would require the military to give notice before bombing a particular target, especially if that target were an American citizen.

legal distinction between ordinary crime and lending support to terrorists.

Most terrorist acts are serious violations of the law of armed conflict. For centuries, international law has recognized a set of rules governing war. The intent of these rules is to limit the use of force to legitimate military goals and to protect civilians and other innocent people. Violations, often referred to as war crimes, include mistreating prisoners of war (POWs), using chemical weapons, and bombing civilian targets such as churches and hospitals. Those charged with war crimes can be tried before a military commission rather than in a criminal court.

The law of armed conflict allows only "lawful combatants"—those who wear uniforms and carry their weapons openly—to kill others. President Bush takes the position that al Qaeda members and other terrorists are unlawful combatants and therefore candidates for military justice. He found support for his stance in a Supreme Court decision, *Ex Parte Quirin*, 317 U.S. 1 (1942), which upheld the military trials of eight Nazi saboteurs found in the United States during World War II.

The Bush administration declared many of the fighters it captured in Afghanistan unlawful combatants and announced its intention to detain them at the Guantanamo Bay Naval Base in Cuba until the end of the conflict. The administration also took steps to hold military trials for those believed to have committed terrorist acts. Even though more than half of the original Guantanamo detainees have been released, the U.S. military considers most of the remaining detainees dangerous and believes that they would rejoin the enemy and try to kill Americans if they were to be released. The administration has also declared at least two American citizens unlawful combatants because they had fought alongside the enemy. They, too, were placed in military custody.

Human rights groups brought legal challenges against the indefinite detention of enemy fighters, and those challenges were partially successful. In *Hamdi v. Rumsfeld*, 542 U.S. 507 (2004), the Supreme Court ruled that an American citizen had the right to challenge his continued detention; and in *Rasul v. Bush*, 542 U.S. 466 (2004), the court concluded that federal law gave the Guantanamo detainees the right to challenge their enemy combatant status. After the court decided *Rasul*, Congress changed the law in question. As a result, the status of Guantanamo detainees is still being argued in the courts.

After September 11, the Bush administration stepped up its efforts to monitor communications involving individuals who live outside the United States and who are suspected of having ties to al Qaeda. The administration justified its surveillance programs as an effort to monitor enemy communications, a long-recognized part of waging war. It also argued that federal laws regulating such surveillance were not only obsolete but also infringed on the president's power as commander in chief of the military. Critics, however, believe that the government is spying on innocent Americans and warn that wide-scale surveillance without oversight by the courts or Congress will lead to abuses.

Unresolved Questions

As the shock of September 11 wore off, some Americans started asking whether their country was taking the right approach toward terrorism. Some believe that the nation's anti-terrorism efforts are setting a bad example for the rest of the world. Others fear that the Bush Doctrine is taking the nation's foreign policy in the wrong direction. They believe that it is contrary to international law and not in the country's long-term best interests, and that it could even make the world more dangerous.

At home, many believe that post–September 11 anti-terrorism laws make it too easy for authorities to spy on citizens, arrest people without good reason, and mistreat minorities. Some also object to the president's assertion of broad wartime powers. They believe that some measures used in past wars were mistakes that should not be repeated, and that presidential powers used to fight world wars are not appropriate in a low-level conflict against a small enemy force.

More than four years after Saddam Hussein's ouster, many Americans now believe that the Iraq war was not worth the lives lost and money spent. Some also believe that the American military presence in Iraq detracts from the fight against those who attacked the United States on September 11, 2001.

Summary

The September 11 attacks marked the beginning of America's war on terror. It is a war in which the enemy is a shadowy organization rather than a hostile country, the objective is hard to define, and fighting could last for many years. The United States has responded to the threat of terrorism by adopting a new foreign policy under which it will strike first to prevent another attack. It has also expanded the government's power to find suspected terrorists and bring them to justice—in some cases, military justice. Some Americans believe that the steps taken to fight terrorism show a lack of respect for the rest of the world and violate traditional American principles of fairness and individual liberty at home.

The United States Must Act Decisively to Defend Itself

The Bush Doctrine, under which the United States will strike enemies before they attack, and, if necessary, act without international approval, has been criticized both at home and abroad. Defenders of the doctrine maintain that a policy of merely reacting to terrorism leaves the country vulnerable to another attack, and that protecting Americans deserves a higher priority than the world's opinion of the United States. As President Bush told the nation in his remarks about the threat posed by Iraq's Saddam Hussein: "Facing clear evidence of peril, we cannot wait for the final proof—the smoking gun—that could come in the form of a mushroom cloud."[1] Supporters of the president's foreign policy also point out that the Bush Doctrine finds support in history: Over the years, the United States has taken preemptive military action against other countries.

The terrorist threat requires a new strategy.

After World War II, the United States was engaged with the Soviet Union in a global struggle known as the Cold War. At the time, the United States had a national security policy based on two principles: One was *deterrence*, which meant the building of a huge arsenal of nuclear weapons that would be launched at the Soviets if they attacked. The other principle was *containment*, which was a combination of military, economic, and diplomatic measures to prevent the spread of communism. Neither the Soviet Union nor the United States wished to start a nuclear war that could destroy all life on Earth. Instead, they indirectly fought one another by supplying arms and other assistance to those fighting small wars in countries such as Afghanistan and Vietnam.

After September 11, the Bush administration concluded that the Cold War strategy that kept the Soviets from attacking would not prevent terrorist attacks. As the 2001 attacks demonstrated, there are people intent on killing Americans and willing to die in the process. Terrorists have also expressed their intention to use weapons of mass destruction against the United States. Some of those weapons, such as "suitcase nukes," are small enough to be smuggled into the country, hidden until needed, and used without warning. Others, such as missiles carrying atomic warheads, can be launched from thousands of miles away and reach their targets in minutes. As President Bush explained, "America is no longer protected by vast oceans. We are protected from attack only by vigorous action abroad, and increased vigilance at home."[2]

There is both reason and precedent for unilateral action.

In the past, a nation knew when a threat was imminent: A fleet of ships was on its way or troops were massing at the border. Under international law, it was then permissible to take military action. In order for terrorist cells to succeed, however, they must operate in secret, and those unseen terrorists might possess weapons capable of killing more people than an entire squadron of World War II bombers. It is therefore necessary to view the concept of "imminent threat" in a new light. As President Bush's 2006 National Security Strategy document explained:

> The greater the threat, the greater is the risk of inaction—and the more compelling the case for taking anticipatory action to defend ourselves, even if uncertainty remains as to the time and place of the enemy's attack. There are few greater threats than a terrorist attack with WMD.[3]

When President Bush called for military action against Iraq, he reminded Americans of the Cuban missile crisis. In October 1962, American intelligence learned that the Soviet Union had built a nuclear missile site in Cuba. President John F. Kennedy responded to the threat immediately by imposing a naval blockade of Cuba to prevent the Soviets from shipping more weapons. The president explained to the nation why he had to act: "We no longer live in a world where only the actual firing of weapons represents a sufficient challenge to a nation's security to constitute maximum peril. Nuclear weapons are so destructive and ballistic missiles are so swift, that any substantially increased possibility of their use or any sudden change in their deployment may well be regarded as a definite threat to peace."[4] Rather than go to war over the missiles, Soviet Premier Nikita Khrushchev agreed to remove them from Cuba in exchange for Kennedy's promise to take American nuclear weapons out of Turkey.

In 1981, Israel took preemptive action to counter the threat of a nuclear attack. After learning that an Iraqi reactor would soon be able to manufacture plutonium, a radioactive element used in bombs, the Israeli air force destroyed it—even though the Iraqis were years away from making a weapon. Richard

Perle, who is now a resident fellow at the American Enterprise Institute, argued that Israel faced an imminent threat. He said: "The Iraqis were about to load fuel into the reactor and once they did so, [Israel] would not have had an opportunity to use an air strike without doing a lot of unintended damage around the facility, because radioactive material would have been released into the atmosphere. . . . They had to deal with a threshold that once crossed, they would no longer have the military option that could be effective at that moment."[5]

It can be argued that the United States faced a similar situation with respect to al Qaeda. The suicide bombings of two

America's "Small War" Against Terror

Over the years, the United States military has been involved in dozens of low-level operations, the objectives of which have ranged from overthrowing dictators to hunting down bandits. These operations typically involved small numbers of troops and no formal declaration of war. They are sometimes referred to as "small wars."

One of America's earliest small wars was against what modern-day politicians would call state-sponsored terrorists. The enemy was the Barbary pirates, who targeted American civilians and were supported by hostile governments. Two hundred years ago, the Barbary States were self-governing provinces of the Turkish Empire. They fought a low-level war against Christian nations in Europe, a war that eventually turned into a protection racket: The Barbary rulers hired pirates to capture ships on the high seas; the ships' crews were held for ransom until payment arrived, and unlucky crewmen were tortured or even sold to slave traders. A number of countries, England in particular, decided that rather than challenge the Barbary rulers, it was cheaper to pay tribute in exchange for safe passage.

Once the United States gained its independence from Great Britain, it no longer enjoyed the protection of the Royal Navy. As a result, American shipping became an easy target for the Barbary pirates. In 1793, after 11 merchant ships had been seized, President Washington considered military action. After European leaders turned down an American proposal for a naval blockade of the Barbary States,

American embassies in August 1998 demonstrated that organization's sophistication and its willingness to inflict mass casualties. Al Qaeda was operating terrorist training camps in Afghanistan and its leader, Osama bin Laden, had already urged his followers to kill Americans. Many observers believe that under those circumstances, there was an imminent danger of an al Qaeda attack and that the United States not only had the right to invade Afghanistan but also should have done so long before al Qaeda attacked Americans on U.S. soil.

The president's supporters maintain that preemptive military action is nothing new. For more than 200 years, U.S.

the United States had little choice but to follow their lead and pay tribute. Those payments were a considerable drain on the federal treasury.

Matters came to a head in 1801, when the new president, Thomas Jefferson, decided to take a hard line against the pirates. He ordered the Navy to blockade the state of Tripolitania, which was harboring the worst of the pirates. He did so against the advice of his attorney general, who believed that only Congress, which was not in session at the time, had the power to declare war. Jefferson was the first of many presidents who believed that he could take military action without congressional approval. A crisis was avoided when Congress authorized him, after the fact, to use "all necessary force" to protect American shipping.

The war with Tripolitania, which was marked by acts of heroism on the part of American seamen, lasted for four years. It ended in May 1805, after a force of Marines and locally recruited Arabs stormed the fortress at Derna and, for the first time, planted the American flag on Old World soil. (The reference to "the shores of Tripoli" in "The Marines' Hymn" comes from that battle.) The American strategy included overthrowing the pasha of Tripolitania and putting his older brother on the throne—the United States's first attempt at "regime change"—but the pasha agreed to peace terms before he could be toppled.

The peace treaty with Tripolitania did not end the United States's troubles with the Barbary pirates; attacks persisted for more than a decade. After the War of 1812, a combination of diplomacy and threats of naval force persuaded the Barbary States to release their American captives and drop their demands for tribute.

presidents have sent the military to punish countries harboring outlaws, remove dictators from office, and restore order to war-torn nations. In 1983, President Ronald Reagan sent a force of Army Rangers and U.S. Marines to Grenada to remove a pro-Communist government from power. Six years later, President George H.W. Bush ordered troops into Panama to arrest its dictator, Manuel Noriega, who was wanted in the United States on drug trafficking charges.

The United States has also gone to war for humanitarian reasons. For example, some people argue that Spain's oppression of the Cuban people was one reason for the Spanish-American War. President Woodrow Wilson, in asking for a declaration of war against Germany (in what would become known as World War I), told Congress that he wanted to make the world "safe for democracy." A recent example of a humanitarian war was the 1999 air war waged by the United States and its North American Treaty Organization (NATO) allies against Serbia. NATO, a military alliance that now includes the United States, Canada, and most of Western Europe, was originally created after World War II to counter the former Soviet Union. NATO's air campaign was successful in forcing the Serbian government to stop its campaign of genocide against ethnic Albanians.

America must be free to defend itself.

Supporters of the invasion of Iraq insist that it was necessary because the United Nations (UN) refused to stop Saddam Hussein from trying to develop WMDs. Backers of the invasion maintain that the UN is not able to stand up to rogue countries, in part because the organization's structure is too cumbersome. On occasion, the UN has approved military action against countries that have committed serious human rights violations. However, the UN Charter makes it possible for a single country to prevent the use of such force. The charter provides that the 15-member Security Council must approve military action. In addition, the charter gives each of the council's 5 permanent members—the United States, Russia, China, France, and the United Kingdom—veto power.

In February 2003, the United States asked the council to authorize military force against Saddam Hussein, and the U.S. ambassador presented evidence that Hussein's government was attempting to produce WMDs. Nevertheless, France and Russia announced their intention to veto a use-of-force resolution. As a result, President Bush organized his own "coalition of the willing."

The stalemate over Iraq also showed that the UN lacks the will to enforce its own resolutions. At the time of the invasion, Hussein was in violation of 16 Security Council resolutions going back to 1991, when he agreed to abandon his weapons program and allow UN inspections in exchange for a cease-fire that halted the Gulf War. Critics warn that if the UN fails to confront scofflaws like Hussein, it will become irrelevant. President Bush said that this happened to the League of Nations in the 1930s: "The League of Nations, lacking both credibility and will, collapsed at the first challenge of the dictators. Free nations failed to recognize, much less confront, the aggressive evil in plain sight. And so dictators went about their business."[6]

The Bush Doctrine's defenders also argue that the United States, as the world's only superpower, has a unique responsibility to protect democracy around the world. It inherited that responsibility from Great Britain, which was the world's mightiest naval power in the nineteenth century. According to Max Boot, a senior fellow at the Council for Foreign Relations:

> Britain battled the "enemies of all mankind," such as pirates and slave traders, and took upon itself the responsibility of keeping the world's oceans and seas open to navigation. . . . Britain acted to preserve the balance of power whenever it was endangered, coming to the aid of weak nations (such as Belgium or Turkey) being bullied by the strong (Germany or Russia).[7]

Where Do We Go From Here? The Iraq Study Group Report

By 2006, public frustration over the Iraq war reached the point that Congress created a commission that would assess the situation in that country. That commission, called the Iraq Study Group, tried to reach a consensus on what must be done in Iraq and also rally the American people behind its recommendations. Panelists worked with the United States Institute of Peace, and consulted with numerous experts and public officials.

The study group's report*, released in late December 2006, called the situation in Iraq "grave and deteriorating," and warned what could happen:

> If the situation continues to deteriorate, the consequences could be severe. A slide toward chaos could trigger the collapse of Iraq's government and a humanitarian catastrophe. Neighboring countries could intervene. Sunni-Shia clashes [between rival religious factions] could spread. Al Qaeda could win a propaganda victory and expand its base of operations. The global standing of the United States could be diminished. Americans could become more polarized.

The panel also concluded that some progress had been made, though. It found that "Iraqis restored full sovereignty, conducted open national elections, drafted a permanent constitution, ratified that constitution, and elected a new government pursuant to that constitution." Still, the panel found much to be concerned about: "Despite a massive effort, stability in Iraq remains elusive and the situation is deteriorating. The Iraqi government cannot now govern, sustain, and defend itself without the support of the United States. Iraqis have not been convinced that they must take responsibility for their own future. Iraq's neighbors and much of the international community have not been persuaded to play an active and constructive role in supporting Iraq."

The study group made a number of suggestions aimed at bringing about President Bush's goal of an Iraq that can "govern itself, sustain itself, and defend itself." In what they called "the external approach," the panelists recommended creating an international support group consisting of Iraq's neighbors as well as key countries around the world. They also called on the United States to negotiate with Iran and Syria, even though the U.S. government considers those regimes hostile; and to renew efforts to resolve the conflict between Israel and the Palestinians. In addition, they advised the United States to refocus on the conflict in Afghanistan, where the Taliban remains a threat.

The panelists also recommended that the United States "help the Iraqis help themselves." They cited a number of steps that the Iraq government had to take, including the following:

- Boosting the size and quality of its military
- Reconciling the country's ethnic and political factions and making efforts to bring insurgent leaders—other than al Qaeda—back into the political system
- Sharing the nation's oil revenue fairly
- Protecting the rights of women, minorities, and non-governmental organizations
- Upgrading the nation's police forces, and rooting out corruption in government ministries that oversee the army and police
- Rebuilding the country's infrastructure and economy and providing jobs for Iraqis
- Building a justice system that respects the rule of law

To accomplish those goals, the panelists urged the United States to offer military support, send skilled personnel to train Iraqi police officers, judges, and intelligence organizations, and provide financial aid to help with reconstruction.

As a short-term measure, the panelists were agreeable to a redeployment, or "surge," of American combat forces to stabilize Baghdad and to speed up the training and equipping mission. In the longer term, they urged the United States to increase the number of American troops embedded in and supporting Iraqi army units and, at the same time, to start to move combat forces out of Iraq.

The panelists said, however, that there were limits to American patience as well as the country's ability to help Iraq if it cannot—or will not—carry out reforms. They urged the United States to work with Iraqi leaders to establish "milestones" for measuring progress, but they also warned: "If the Iraqi government fails to make such progress, the U.S. should reduce its political, military, or economic support for that government."

* James A. Baker, III, and Lee H. Hamilton, co-chairs, *The Iraq Study Group Report: The Way Forward—A New Approach.* New York: Random House, 2006.

In recent years, the United States has taken the lead in stopping genocide in the former Yugoslavia as well as battling weapons suppliers and drug traffickers.

Diplomacy is usually preferable to war, but it does not always succeed. One of history's most famous examples of diplomatic failure was the efforts of European leaders to appease Adolf Hitler. In 1938, Hitler demanded that a portion of Czechoslovakia called the Sudetenland be handed over to Germany. Great Britain, France, and Italy agreed to give Hitler the Sudetenland in exchange for his promise not to demand any more territory. After the deal, British Prime Minister Neville Chamberlain said he had brought "peace in our time." Chamberlain was wrong. Hitler took over the rest of Czechoslovakia and later invaded Poland, forcing the Allies to go to war to stop him. Military historian Victor Davis Hanson argues that *not* going to war is often the deadlier option:

> The three greatest scourges of the twentieth century—Nazism, Japanese militarism, and Soviet Communism—were defeated through war or continued military resistance. More were killed by Hitler, Stalin, and Mao outside of combat than died in World Wars I and II. . . . Wickedness—whether chattel slavery, the gas chambers, or concentration camps—has rarely passed into the night on its own. The present evil [of terrorism] isn't going to either.[8]

Sometimes a country has no choice but to act first. When the costs of taking action are high but the benefits are widely shared—as in the case of eliminating a dangerous dictator—smaller countries are understandably reluctant to make the first move. In those situations, it becomes the responsibility of the United States to mobilize the rest of the world. Another problem is that other countries do not take the threat of terrorism as seriously as does the United States. In 2003, Richard Perle remarked, "I would be surprised if someone over coffee and apple cake in

Oslo would feel similarly threatened. So we shouldn't expect our European friends and allies to share the sense of apprehension that we have as a result of September 11th."[9]

Finally, supporters of the Bush Doctrine argue that it is unacceptable for unelected foreign bureaucrats to control America's foreign policy. As Vice President Dick Cheney explained, "To accept the view that action by America and our allies can be stopped by the objection of foreign governments that may not feel threatened is to confer undue power on them, while leaving the rest of us powerless to act in our own defense."[10] The president's supporters also insist that the United Nations has no business dictating U.S. foreign policy: The UN Charter does not trump the U.S. Constitution, which obligates the president to provide for the common defense.

Many supporters are also disturbed by a trend toward world government, which could do more harm than good. The biggest concern is that international bodies will regulate American military power, reducing the president's ability to defend the country from dictators and aggressors. Former Justice Department lawyers David Rivkin and Lee Casey, who strongly support the administration's policies, warn, "If the trends of international law in the 1990s are allowed to mature into binding rules, international law will prove to be one of the most potent weapons ever deployed against the United States."[11] Some even warn that hostile regimes will someday try to prosecute American military commanders, even the president himself, on trumped-up charges of war crimes.

The Bush Doctrine succeeded in Iraq.

The president's 2006 National Security Strategy reasserted that a strategy based on deterrence no longer protects the country, and that sometimes the United States will be forced to act first to stop an enemy from attacking. Those principles required the United States to use military force to deal with Iraq. David

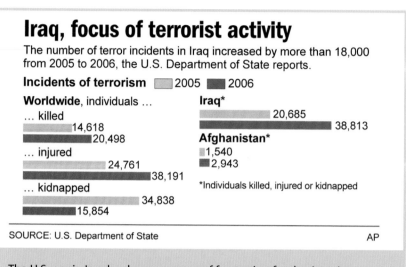

Iraq, focus of terrorist activity

The number of terror incidents in Iraq increased by more than 18,000 from 2005 to 2006, the U.S. Department of State reports.

Incidents of terrorism ▦ 2005 ▉ 2006

Worldwide, individuals ...
... killed
14,618
20,498
... injured
24,761
38,191
... kidnapped
34,838
15,854

Iraq*
20,685
38,813

Afghanistan*
1,540
2,943

*Individuals killed, injured or kidnapped

SOURCE: U.S. Department of State   AP

The U.S. war in Iraq has been a source of frustration for the American public. Since Saddam Hussein was officially deposed and captured, it has been difficult to see any progress being made in the country. The chart above shows that the number of terror incidents in Iraq increased from 2005 to 2006.

Frum and Richard Perle of the American Enterprise Institute explained why it was necessary to go to war:

> We knew that Iraq had almost certainly built additional weapons, weapons components, and weapons materials in the 1990s. We knew that Iraq retained the skills and knowledge to build biological and nuclear weapons. We knew that Saddam Hussein desperately wanted those weapons. We knew that it was only a matter of time before he would regain the resources to acquire them.[12]

The president's supporters also argue that not invading Iraq would have sent the wrong message to the enemy—namely, that the country is willing to fight low-intensity wars but shies away from riskier conflicts. They add that now that the United States is in Iraq, it is imperative that insurgent forces there be defeated. Max Boot explained:

> If we are seen as the losers in Iraq, al Qaeda would be seen as the winner. The perception of American weakness fed by a pullout would lead to increased terrorism against the U.S. and our allies, just as occurred following our withdrawal from Somalia in 1993 and from Beirut in 1983.
>
> In the ensuing chaos, it is quite possible that al Qaeda terrorists would succeed in turning western Iraq into a Taliban-style base for international terrorism.[13]

Many believe that a show of strength is the only way to force foreign heads of state to cooperate with the United States. One example is Pakistan President Pervez Musharraf, who not only backed the Taliban regime but also relied on "graduates" of al Qaeda's training camps to fight against India before September 11. After the attacks, Secretary of State Colin Powell warned Musharraf to renounce terrorism or else face the consequences. Musharraf abandoned the Taliban, fired pro-Taliban officers from the army and intelligence service, and confronted Pakistani militants he had previously supported.

Those who support the Iraq war contend that it did more than remove a dangerous dictator from power. After Saddam Hussein's ousting, Libyan dictator Muammar Qaddafi abandoned his weapons of mass destruction, and Iran's regime decided to allow weapons inspectors into its country. Supporters also argue that the invasion could pay dividends in the long term. If the war results in a stable and democratic Iraq, other governments in the region would be forced to take steps to make their societies more democratic and less hostile to the United States.

Summary

The most important responsibility a country owes its citizens is protecting them from the country's enemies. The

September 11 attacks forced the United States to shift its national security strategy from retaliating after an attack to preventing one from happening in the first place. Supporters of the Bush

Bringing War Criminals to Justice

International criminal law has existed for centuries, but until recently, only countries were believed to have the power to punish violators. That notion changed after World War II. As the war neared an end, Allied leaders debated what to do with Adolf Hitler and other top Nazi officials. British Prime Minister Winston Churchill favored summarily executing them all. The United States proposed an alternative: trying the Nazis for war crimes before an international court. American officials believed that trials would identify the guilty individuals and expose their crimes to the world. The other Allies agreed to create an international tribunal to try alleged war criminals.

The tribunal, which consisted of judges from France, Great Britain, the Soviet Union, and the United States, met in Nuremberg, Germany, the city where the Nazis held their party rallies and enacted the notorious racial classification laws. In November 1945, the first trial began. It focused on major war criminals (lower-ranking officials were tried later). The defendants were charged with traditional violations of the law of armed conflict as well as two new offenses, "crimes against peace" and "crimes against humanity," which are now recognized in international law. The trials were governed by procedures that resembled those followed in American criminal cases, except that there was no jury trial and no appeal.

In October 1946, after hearing more than 200 days of testimony, the judges returned their verdicts. They found 19 defendants guilty and sentenced 12 to death, 3 to life in prison, and 4 to lesser prison terms. They found 3 defendants not guilty. The judges rejected the argument that only a state, and not an individual, could be guilty of war crimes. They also rejected the argument that a person was not guilty if he was only following orders, a plea now called the "Nuremberg defense." Legal experts generally believe that the Nuremberg trials were fair, although it can be argued that some of the charges were *ex post facto*, meaning that actions were defined as crimes after the fact. Like other war crimes trials, though, Nuremberg has been criticized as "victor's justice," as no top Allied leaders were tried for war crimes.

Doctrine believe that international organizations such as the United Nations are neither able nor willing to confront dictators. They insist that the United States, as the world's only military

---

After Nuremburg, some members of the United Nations proposed a permanent war crimes tribunal, but the Cold War stalemate between the United States and the Soviet Union prevented its creation for the time being. Then, in 1993, the UN Security Council created a special tribunal to prosecute those responsible for "ethnic cleansing" and other war crimes in Bosnia. It was the first such court to prosecute a head of state, former Serbian president Slobodan Milosevic, and was also the first to recognize rape as a war crime. The Security Council later established tribunals to prosecute war crimes committed in the African nations of Rwanda and Sierra Leone.

In 1998, delegates at a UN-sponsored conference in Rome voted overwhelmingly in favor of creating a permanent International Criminal Court with jurisdiction over cases of genocide, crimes against humanity, and violations of the law of armed conflict. The treaty took effect on July 1, 2002.

The International Criminal Court is a "court of last resort," one that may act only when the country with primary responsibility either cannot or will not prosecute. It is aimed at regimes such as that of Pol Pot in Cambodia (1976–1979), where there was no independent justice system. Supporters of the court believe that a permanent institution is less likely to dispense victor's justice because the list of offenses has been drawn up in advance and the judges and prosecutors are already in place.

Nevertheless, the United States is concerned that members of its armed forces, which are stationed in more than 100 countries around the world, could become targets of politically motivated prosecutions for war crimes. It voted against creating the court and has asked its allies and the UN Security Council to give American service members immunity from prosecution.

Supporters of the court believe that American fears are exaggerated, pointing out that there are safeguards against unfair prosecutions and that Americans charged with war crimes can be tried under the U.S. system of military justice. In fact, the military has prosecuted American soldiers who were accused of killing or mistreating civilians while serving in Iraq. Court supporters add that by rejecting the court's jurisdiction, the United States finds itself in the company of such rogue nations as Burma, Cuba, and North Korea.

superpower, has a unique responsibility to fight terrorism and protect human rights. They warn that other countries' attempts to regulate the United States's use of military power will encourage terrorists and enable dictators to defy the rest of the world. In addition, President Bush's supporters argue that he made the right decision by using force to oust Saddam Hussein rather than waiting for the dictator to re-acquire and use weapons of mass destruction.

Unilateralism and Preemptive War Do More Harm Than Good

America's war on terror began with broad international support: The North Atlantic Treaty Organization (NATO) declared that the September 11 attacks were attacks on all of its members, and the United Nations Security Council unanimously passed a resolution supporting "international efforts to root out terrorism" in Afghanistan.[1] That resolution effectively approved the American-led invasion. More recently, however, the United States has been at odds with much of the world over its foreign policy, especially after it waged a preemptive war against Iraq without UN approval and over the objections of much of the international community.

The Iraq war is part of a larger controversy surrounding the Bush Doctrine, which emphasizes unilateral and preemptive military action, along with "regime change": taking steps,

including the use of military force, to overthrow hostile governments. Critics believe that such a policy will create even worse
problems than those the Bush administration is trying to solve.

The Bush Doctrine raises legal and ethical concerns.

After World War II, world leaders tried to prevent future wars
by establishing international rules restricting the use of force.
The war crimes trials at Nuremberg, Germany, recognized
aggression—going to war without justification—as a war crime,
and the United Nations Charter, which the United States signed,
obligated its members to use force only in self-defense.

Some believe that the United States, by leading an invasion
of Iraq, abused its right to defend itself. The Defense Department defines a "preemptive war" as "an attack initiated on
the basis of incontrovertible evidence that an enemy attack is
imminent," and a "preventive war" as an attack "initiated in the
belief that military conflict, while not imminent, is inevitable,
and that to delay would involve greater risk."[2] A preemptive
war is generally considered legitimate, but a preventive war is
not. In fact, some find it hard to distinguish a preventive war
from a war of aggression. Some experts believe that the Iraq
war was preventive because Saddam Hussein did not pose an
imminent threat to the United States. Before the war, a panel
of New York City lawyers found that "Iraq has not, since the
end of the 1991 Gulf War, used force or directly threatened
the United States (aside from attacks on allied airplanes in the
no-fly zones). Logically, any threat that Iraq poses is not of an
immediate nature."[3]

Finally, opponents argue that the Bush Doctrine increases
the risk that the United States will go to war on a mistaken
assumption. There is evidence that this happened in Iraq. After
the invasion, a team of weapons inspectors called the Iraq Survey
Group concluded that Saddam Hussein did not have WMDs—
the main reason why the United States went to war. Some critics,

such as Joseph Wilson IV, the former senior director of African Affairs for the National Security Council, believed that the Bush administration rushed to judgment about Iraq's WMD program. Wilson, a former U.S. ambassador, traveled to the African country of Niger to investigate claims that Saddam Hussein attempted to buy uranium, an element that is used in atomic weapons. He concluded that the claims were unfounded. Nevertheless, President Bush told the nation in his 2003 State of the Union address, "The British government has learned that Saddam Hussein recently sought significant quantities of uranium from Africa."[4] After the invasion of Iraq, Wilson wrote a column in the *New York Times* in which he said:

> If my information was deemed inaccurate, I understand (though I would be very interested to know why). If, however, the information was ignored because it did not fit certain preconceptions about Iraq, then a legitimate argument can be made that we went to war under false pretenses.[5]

Unilateral military action makes the world more dangerous.

A foreign policy that relies on military power and seeks regime change overseas could leave the world—the United States included—a more dangerous place in the long run. Some believe that the Bush Doctrine will encourage other countries to speed up their nuclear weapons programs in an effort to ward off an American invasion. Michael Ignatieff, who was a professor specializing in human rights issues before he was elected to the Canadian parliament, wrote, "To date, the only factor that keeps the United States from intervening is if the country in question has nuclear weapons. . . . No wonder a Pakistani general is supposed to have remarked in 1999 that the chief lesson he drew from the display of American precision air power in Kosovo was for his country to acquire nuclear weapons as quickly as possible."[6]

There is also concern that America's policy of preemptive military action might encourage other countries to attack their long-time enemies. India and Pakistan have gone to war several times in the past and recently came close to fighting another war

When Can the President Wage War?

The framers of the Constitution, who did not want the United States to be ruled by a king, divided war powers between the president and Congress. Article II, Section 2 of the Constitution makes the president commander in chief of the armed forces, but Article I, Section 8, Clause 11 gives Congress the power to declare war.

The lack of a clear dividing line between presidential and congressional powers has led to a long-running political debate, as well as occasional lawsuits to stop pending wars. (A war does not require a formal declaration. In fact, only five American wars were ever declared.) Presidents have contended that the commander-in-chief power is broad enough to go to war without congressional approval. Many lawmakers and legal scholars believe that the framers of the Constitution intended to limit the president's war-making power to "repelling sudden attacks." So far, the courts have avoided facing the issue head-on, citing a number of reasons why it would be inappropriate to act. Cases from recent wars include these:

Massachusetts v. Laird, 451 F.2d 26 (1st Cir. 1971). A federal appeals court found that Congress effectively approved the Vietnam War by repeatedly voting to keep funding it. As a result, the court found that Congress and the president had not taken opposite positions on the war, which left it with no clear issue to decide.

Dellums v. Bush, 752 F. Supp. 1141 (D.D.C. 1990). A federal district court rejected a challenge to the Gulf War because the issue was not yet "ripe." The court found that the president had not made a final decision to go to war, and that Congress had yet to vote on a resolution authorizing military force. (It would pass such a resolution days before the war began.)

Doe v. Bush, 323 F.3d 133 (1st Cir. 2003). A federal appeals court refused to stop the invasion of Iraq, finding that no "case or controversy" had arisen because last-minute diplomacy still could avert war. The court suggested

over the disputed territory of Kashmir. North Korea has threatened to attack South Korea. China has threatened to invade Taiwan if Taiwan declares its independence. All of those potential aggressors have nuclear weapons.

that a case or controversy might exist if Congress gave the president a "blank check" to wage war or if the president ordered military action in defiance of a congressional resolution.

The dispute between branches of government is further complicated by the War Powers Resolution (50 U.S.C. §§1541–1548), which Congress passed over President Richard Nixon's veto in 1973. The act requires the president to notify Congress within 48 hours after taking military action and requires congressional approval if the campaign lasts longer than 60 days. Nixon, and the presidents who followed him, believed that this resolution was unconstitutional but nevertheless acted consistently with its requirements.

So far, the courts have avoided ruling on the resolution's constitutionality. In *Campbell v. Clinton*, 203 F.3d 19 (D.C. Cir. 2000), some members of Congress sued President Clinton, alleging that he had violated the War Powers Resolution by continuing the Kosovo war past the 60-day deadline. The Court of Appeals refused to decide the case, ruling that Congress still had legislative means of ending the conflict, such as ordering an end to the war or refusing to approve funds for it. It added that Congress had sent a mixed message about Kosovo because the House voted to fund operations there and defeated a resolution ordering the president to end the war immediately.

According to legal commentator John Dean, "Scholars agree that *Campbell v. Clinton* largely ended all hope of using the federal courts to hold the president accountable under a constitutional requirement that Congress must declare or authorize war before a president can engage in war."* Dean pointed out, however, that Congress could stop a war by cutting off funding; it did so in 1974, forcing President Nixon to end America's involvement in Vietnam.

*John W. Dean, "Pursuant to the Constitution and Despite Claims to the Contrary, President Bush Needs Congressional Approval Before Declaring War on Iraq." http://writ.news.findlaw.com/dean/20020830.html.

Critics of the Bush Doctrine worry that even though pre-emptive military action might have short-term benefits, it creates serious problems in the long run. Richard Falk, a professor emeritus of international law at Princeton University, warns that the fight against terror "is a war in which the pursuit of the traditional military goal of 'victory' is almost certain to intensify the challenge and spread the violence."[7] One likely consequence of invading another country is a guerrilla war—a lesson the Soviets learned in Afghanistan. George McGovern, the Democratic Party's 1972 nominee for president, and William R. Polk, a professor and foreign policy consultant, argued in their book *Out of Iraq* that using military power to bring democracy to other countries is likely to fail. They explain:

> "Nation building" has been a failure: a study by Minxin Pei and Sara Kasper of the Carnegie Endowment for International Peace examined 16 instances aimed at converting the natives to "the American way." Eleven of the sixteen were outright failures and only two, in tiny and nearby societies, were unambiguous successes.[8]

The authors added that even citizens of dictatorships have fought, often ferociously, to drive out foreign invaders.

Sir Michael Howard, a British military historian, believes that the United States should learn from his country's experience with terrorists. He wrote:

> In the intricate game of skill played between terrorists and the authorities, as the British discovered in both Palestine and Ireland, the terrorists have already won an important battle if they can provoke the authorities into using overt armed force against them. They will then be in a win-win situation: either they will escape to fight another day, or they will be defeated and celebrated as martyrs.[9]

The Bush Doctrine has made America weaker.

Some observers maintain that the Bush Doctrine commits the United States to a permanent conflict with the rest of the world. Historian Geoffrey Perret explains:

> However rich they become, neither the Europeans, the Russians, nor the Chinese will become direct rivals of the United States. They will nibble U.S. supremacy down to a nub, with American help: military interventions in poor countries pave the road to exhaustion. The [National Security Strategies of] 2002 and 2006 provide the road map for getting there.
>
> While the United States, with its post-9/11 sense of victimhood, trundles angrily down that road, the Europeans will devote themselves to shoring up what remains of the West while the Chinese continue to pursue what they see as their predestined role to dominate East Asia and recover Taiwan. The struggle for tomorrow's world will not be military, but political, cultural, and, above all, economic.[10]

Many critics believe that the Iraq war has hurt America's fight against terrorism. Daniel Benjamin and Steven Simon contend that the administration's obsession with Saddam Hussein distracted it from taking such needed steps as securing the nation's infrastructure, preventing the smuggling of WMDs into this country, developing a strategy for responding to a biological attack, and monitoring who is entering and leaving the United States. The Iraq war has also consumed money that could have been put to better use elsewhere. In 2008, shortly before the fifth anniversary of the Iraq invasion, economists Linda Bilmes and Joseph Stiglitz told a congressional committee that the total cost of the war would be at least $3 trillion.

Some believe that the invasion and occupation of Iraq has actually played into al Qaeda's hands. James Fallows, the national correspondent for *Atlantic Monthly* magazine, observed:

So far the war in Iraq has advanced the jihadist cause because it generates a steady supply of Islamic victims, or martyrs; because it seems to prove Osama bin Laden's contention that America lusts to occupy Islam's sacred sites, abuse Muslim people, and steal Muslim resources; and because it raises the tantalizing possibility that humble Muslim insurgents, with cheap, primitive weapons, can once more hobble and ultimately destroy a superpower, as they believe they did to the Soviet Union in Afghanistan twenty years ago.[11]

America has become a bad international citizen.

The Bush Doctrine has added to a perception overseas that the United States has become a law unto itself. Since the end of the Cold War, this country has increasingly defied the rest of the world, rejecting the Convention on the Rights of the Child, the Law of the Sea Treaty, the Kyoto Protocol on global climate change, the Anti-Landmine Convention, and the International Criminal Court (ICC). The United States not only voted against creating the ICC, but also considers it illegitimate and has taken steps to defeat its jurisdiction. Many believe that by walking away from the court, the United States wasted its chance to persuade other countries to improve it.

Critics also accuse the United States of inconsistency in its dealings with international bodies. The International Court of Justice (World Court) is one example. After the 1979 Iranian Revolution, the United States obtained a judgment condemning Iran's holding of American hostages. Later, however, the United States argued that the World Court had no jurisdiction to hear Nicaragua's complaint that American forces mined its harbors. Some believe that such behavior sets a bad example, encouraging other countries to ignore their international commitments as well.

Opponents of the Bush Doctrine believe that by ignoring the international community, the United States not only squandered the world's sympathy toward it—the French newspaper *Le*

Monde ran the famous headline, "We Are All Americans," after September 11—but also inflamed anti-American sentiment, especially in the Middle East. Less than two years after September 11, a Pew Research study found that foreigners' attitudes toward the United States had turned strongly negative. Anti-American feeling might, in the long run, encourage other countries to form alliances aimed at keeping this country in check.

America still needs allies.

The United States is the world's only superpower, but it is still in its long-term best interest to work with the rest of the world to fight terror as well as other national security threats such as global warming and infectious diseases. Even if viewed purely from an economic standpoint, the United States still needs the support of other countries: Acting alone costs money. As Michael Ignatieff observed, "Where U.S. interventions have had perceived legitimacy and coalition support—in Bosnia, Kosovo, and Afghanistan—the U.S. has been able to share burdens, transfer costs, and begin to plan an exit. In Iraq, it will bear the costs mostly alone, without an exit in sight."[12] In the 1991 Gulf War against Iraq, the United States acted with UN approval and persuaded its allies to contribute toward the cost of that war. In contrast, the only country that made a significant military commitment to the 2003 war was Great Britain, which has since reduced its presence there. Some traditional allies, including France and Germany, refused to send troops. Meanwhile, the international community has been slow to contribute financial aid toward Iraq's reconstruction.

Ignatieff further believes that the United States has forgotten that reality:

> It is dependent on Mexico and Canada to keep its border secure; it needs Europe's police forces to track terrorist cells in the Islamic diaspora. It cannot contain the North Korean nuclear threat without the Chinese, Japanese, and South

Koreans. Preventing the Pakistani regime from collapsing and its nuclear weapons from falling into terrorist hands depends on the cooperation of the Indian government.[13]

He also warns, "Without friends and allies, a war against terror will fail."[14]

After World War II, the United States and its allies benefited from working together. Notable successes include the United Nations; the Marshall Plan, which helped rebuild Europe; and NATO, which contained the Soviet Union. They made allies of former enemies and set the stage for victory in the Cold War.

A foreign policy that stresses overseas intervention—especially in the pursuit of loosely defined goals such as fighting terrorism and promoting democracy—creates the risk that the United States will overextend itself, a mistake that many historians believe

Use of Force: Article 51 of the UN Charter

Article 51 of the United Nations Charter spells out a nation's right to use military action to defend itself. It provides:

> Nothing in the present Charter shall impair the inherent right of individual or collective self-defence [sic] if an armed attack occurs against a Member of the United Nations, until the Security Council has taken measures necessary to maintain international peace and security. Measures taken by Members in the exercise of this right of self-defence shall be immediately reported to the Security Council and shall not in any way affect the authority and responsibility of the Security Council under the present Charter to take at any time such action as it deems necessary in order to maintain or restore international peace and security.

David Frum and Richard Perle of the American Enterprise Institute, who are highly critical of the UN, consider Article 51 a relic of an era when the greatest threat to world peace was an armed invasion of one country by another country's

led to the fall of the Roman Empire. Military experts warn that the American military is already overstretched by fighting simultaneous wars in Afghanistan and Iraq and against terrorists worldwide. The strain on U.S. forces has become so serious that in August 2007, a top military adviser to President Bush suggested that the time had come to think about reinstating the military draft.

Finally, the international community understands that "non-state actors" such as drug cartels, arms proliferators, and terrorists threaten global security and require collective action. In fact, the UN has taken steps in the fight against terrorism. After the September 11 attacks, the Security Council passed Resolution 1373, one of its strongest ever. This resolution calls on member countries to crack down on terrorists inside their borders and to make it illegal to provide financial aid to terrorist organizations. Although the UN is unpopular with many Americans, it is highly

---

armed forces. Frum and Perle argue that only that kind of an invasion meets Article 51's definition of an "armed attack" that justifies military action in self-defense. They explain:

> It is not an "armed attack" against the United States when Syria sends money and weapons to Hezbollah, even though Hezbollah has attacked Americans in the past and will almost certainly do so in the future. Nor is it an "armed attack" on the United States if Pakistan shares its nuclear technology with North Korea, although a North Korean nuclear bomb would constitute an extremely grave threat to the United States. Nor yet is it an "armed attack" for Iran to grant refuge to al Qaeda terrorists, although al Qaeda is daily plotting to murder Americans by the thousands.*

The authors propose amending Article 51 to provide that harboring, supporting, or financing terrorists is an act of aggression in itself.

* David Frum and Richard Perle, *An End to Evil: How to Win the War on Terror.* New York: Random House, 2003: p. 269.

regarded overseas and can open doors that the United States cannot. In fact, some Islamic countries, as well as the Association of Southeast Asian Nations (ASEAN), stated that they would take part in a campaign against terrorism only if it is carried out under UN leadership.

Summary

The Bush Doctrine, which contemplates unilateral American action, even without the approval of other countries, has alienated much of the world and might violate international law. The doctrine also makes the world more dangerous by encouraging countries to invade their neighbors and to acquire nuclear weapons in order to head off an invasion. Iraq demonstrated that the doctrine breeds anti-American sentiment, insurgency, and terrorism. As powerful as the United States is, it still needs allies to combat a range of security threats. Its refusal to abide by international treaties and work with bodies such as the UN could lead other countries to not cooperate with, or even oppose, American efforts to fight terrorism.

Military Justice Is an Appropriate Way to Deal with Terrorists

After the September 11 attacks, the United States and its allies took thousands of enemy fighters into custody. Most surrendered or were captured during the invasion of Afghanistan, but others were apprehended by intelligence and law enforcement agencies. The president detained hundreds of them as unlawful combatants. He found support for his actions in a long-established principle of the law of armed conflict, which Supreme Court Justice Sandra Day O'Connor explained in *Hamdi v. Rumsfeld*, 2004:

> Captivity is neither a punishment nor an act of vengeance, but merely a temporary detention which is devoid of all penal character.... A prisoner of war is no convict; his imprisonment is a simple war measure.... The object of

capture is to prevent the captured individual from serving the enemy. He is disarmed and from then on must be
removed as completely as practicable from the front, treated
humanely, and in time exchanged, repatriated, or otherwise
released.[1]

The president also announced his intention to try accused war
criminals before military commissions instead of ordinary criminal courts. His actions were consistent with American military
history and court opinions arising out of earlier conflicts. The
president's supporters argue that military justice for terrorists
will better protect this country from future attacks.

America is at war.

Legal experts agree that the September 11 attacks—a mass
murder of mostly civilians by enemy fighters disguised as
civilians—were an act of war. As the 9/11 Commission pointed
out, al Qaeda had been at war with the United States since at
least 1998 when its leader, Osama bin Laden, advocated killing
American civilians.

After the September 11 attacks, the United States went to
war. Congress did not formally declare war, but it did pass a resolution authorizing the president to take military action against
those responsible for the attacks. Even though the war on terror differs from past conflicts, the president has the same constitutional duty as other wartime presidents: to provide for the
common defense. Article II, Section 2 of the U.S. Constitution
makes the president the commander in chief of the armed forces.
Therefore, it is ultimately his decision where to send troops, how
to attack the enemy, and what to do with enemy fighters who
surrender or are captured. During World War II, Supreme Court
Chief Justice Harlan Stone stated, "The war power of the national
government is 'the power to wage war successfully.' . . . It extends
to every matter and activity so related to war as substantially to
affect its conduct and progress. The power is not restricted to

Military Commissions and the Constitution:
Ex Parte Milligan and *Ex Parte Quirin*

During the Civil War, military authorities arrested thousands of civilians living in the North on charges of disloyalty to the Union government. Many were tried by military commissions.

In 1864, a Union spy uncovered a plot by Southern sympathizers to stage an uprising in Indiana. Lamdin Milligan and four alleged co-conspirators were arrested, tried by a military commission, and sentenced to death. Even though President Andrew Johnson commuted their sentence to life in prison, Milligan and his co-defendants filed a habeas corpus petition in federal court. They argued that a military commission had no authority to try them.

The case reached the Supreme Court, which in *Ex Parte Milligan*, 71 U.S.2 (1866), ordered the prisoners' release. All nine justices agreed that the Bill of Rights was not suspended during wartime and that the prisoners should not have been tried by a military commission. Although they agreed on this point, they disagreed on the reason for their decision. Justice David Davis, writing for the five-member majority, concluded that a military trial was unconstitutional under the circumstances. He pointed out that Milligan and his fellow defendants were not in the armed forces, and that Indiana was neither in a state of rebellion nor under invasion by the Confederate Army.

Even though the Habeas Corpus Act of 1863, which authorized the government to detain accused criminals without charging them, was constitutional, Chief Justice Salmon Chase concluded that military justice was not. He stated: "Martial rule can never exist where the courts are open, and in the proper and unobstructed exercise of their jurisdiction. It is also confined to the locality of actual war."

Four justices, led by Salmon P. Chase, agreed with the result, but argued that the case should have been decided on a narrower issue. In their concurring opinion, they contended that the government had violated the Habeas Corpus Act by not freeing Milligan and his fellow defendants after the Indiana grand jury finished its term without charging them with any crimes. Chase also suggested that there might come a time when Congress would determine that civilian courts were incapable of hearing cases involving national security. He wrote: "Those courts might be open and undisturbed in the execution of their functions, and

(continues)

(continued)

yet wholly incompetent to avert threatened danger, or to punish, with adequate promptitude and certainty, the guilty conspirators."

The Supreme Court did not revisit the issue of military trials until World War II, when federal authorities arrested eight Nazi agents who had been sent to the United States to commit sabotage. The defendants filed a habeas corpus petition alleging that the government had no authority to try them before a commission. Their case quickly reached the Supreme Court, which, in *Ex Parte Quirin*, 317 U.S. 1 (1942), unanimously upheld the constitutionality of their military trials.

Chief Justice Harlan Stone wrote the court's opinion. He concluded that the Articles of War passed by Congress authorized military trials for violators of the law of armed conflict. In this case, after the men came ashore in the United States, they took off their German military uniforms and put on civilian clothes. By fighting without wearing "fixed and distinctive emblems," they became "unlawful combatants." Justice Stone explained:

> Lawful combatants are subject to capture and detention as prisoners of war by opposing military forces. Unlawful combatants are likewise subject to capture and detention, but in addition they are subject to trial and punishment by military tribunals for acts which render their belligerency unlawful. The spy ... or an enemy combatant who without uniform comes secretly through the lines for the purpose of waging war by destruction of life or property, are familiar examples of belligerents who are generally deemed not to be entitled to the status of prisoners of war, but to be offenders against the law of war subject to trial and punishment by military tribunals.

Justice Stone also rejected the argument that American citizens could not be tried by commissions. He wrote, "Citizenship in the United States of an enemy belligerent does not relieve him from the consequences of a belligerency which is unlawful because [it is] in violation of the law of war."

In addition, the chief justice concluded that *Ex Parte Milligan* did not bar military trials in this case. He explained that Lamdin Milligan, "not being a part of or associated with the armed forces of the enemy, was a non-belligerent, not subject to the law of war." One question not answered by *Quirin* is whether the president, as commander in chief of the armed forces, has the inherent power to try enemy fighters before a commission. That question remains unanswered. In *Hamdan v. Rumsfeld*, 2006, the court concluded that Congress had authorized President Bush to create military commissions.

the winning of victories in the field and the repulse of enemy forces."[2]

In times of war, courts generally refuse to substitute their judgment for that of the president. There are good reasons for this policy. Wartime decisions must be made swiftly, often on the basis of incomplete or conflicting information, and the president is accountable to voters, while judges are not. When new enemies such as al Qaeda confront the United States, it is important that the president be given flexibility in deciding how to fight them. As Justice Clarence Thomas stated in his dissent in *Hamdan v. Rumsfeld*, 2006: "The Court's evident belief that *it* is qualified to pass on the '[m]ilitary necessity'... of the Commander in Chief's decision to employ a particular form of force against our enemies is so antithetical to our constitutional structure that it simply cannot go unanswered."[3]

Military justice is a legitimate wartime measure.

Although the invasion of Afghanistan was in many ways a conventional war, al Qaeda is a new kind of enemy. Its members fight for a cause rather than a specific country, rely on secrecy and deception, and plan acts of terrorism while living among their victims. Al Qaeda fighters have also repeatedly violated the law of armed combat by attacking civilians, not wearing identifying insignia, and not carrying their weapons openly. Therefore, like the saboteurs in *Quirin*, they are unlawful combatants who can be tried by a military commission for war crimes.

The U.S. military has detained more than 700 enemy combatants at Guantanamo, and about half of them are still there. Even though their legal status is still unresolved, the Supreme Court reaffirmed in *Hamdi v. Rumsfeld*, 2004, that the commander in chief of the military has the right to detain enemy fighters. Two years later, in *Hamdan*, 2006, the Court upheld the use of military commissions in general, even though it found procedural flaws in the commissions created by President Bush.

After the 9/11 attacks, the United States took into custody many enemy combatants in Iraq and elsewhere. The Department of Defense maintained that military justice—that is, the use of military courts and the military code of law—is an appropriate way to deal with these prisoners. Above, a Department of Defense official explains the rules that will be used in trying terrorist suspects.

Supporters maintain that the indefinite detention of enemy fighters is a better alternative than summarily killing them on the battlefield. David Rivkin and Lee Casey explain:

> The right to detain captured enemy combatants, without trial, without lawyers, and without an established release schedule, stems from one of the most important humanitarian advances in the law of armed conflict, dating back at

least to the 17th century—the rise of an obligation to "give quarter." Before this, except for a few wealthy or powerful individuals worth ransoming, captured soldiers could be, and very often were, put to the sword.[4]

There are other justifications for detaining enemy fighters. Some fighters, especially high-ranking members of al Qaeda, have valuable intelligence about their organization and could provide information that will help the United States stop future terrorist attacks. In addition, detaining suspected terrorists makes it less likely that they can communicate with those terrorists who are still at large.

In any event, the government has taken steps to make sure that innocent people are not being detained at Guantanamo. After the *Rasul* decision, it created Combatant Status Review Tribunals (CSRTs) that determine whether non-citizens detained outside the United States should remain in captivity. Every detainee has had at least one tribunal hearing, and more than 30 detainees were freed after the first round of hearings took place. The government argues that the tribunals give detainees the due process of law they asked for in the *Rasul* case, and therefore it is no longer necessary for courts to second-guess the military's decisions regarding their status.

The criminal justice system cannot deal with terrorism.

Because the September 11 attacks were acts of war, experts such as former White House lawyer Bradford Berenson insist, "A person making war on the U.S. who seeks to slaughter thousands of our citizens in the streets must face our military, not our judges."[5] There is a difference between fighting a war and pursuing common criminals. Not even the strongest critics of military justice believe that American troops need a warrant to search Osama bin Laden's hideout, or that they must read captured al Qaeda fighters their Miranda warnings before questioning them.

There are several reasons why the criminal justice system cannot deal effectively with terrorism. To begin with, it focuses on punishing criminals after the fact and is therefore not well-suited

Hamdan v. Rumsfeld: Is Military Justice Fair?

Salim Hamdan was captured during the invasion of Afghanistan and detained as an enemy combatant at Guantanamo. While he was there, President Bush determined that he was possibly guilty of war crimes and therefore eligible for trial before a military commission. Eventually, Hamdan was charged with conspiracy to commit terrorist acts and with several overt acts in advancing the conspiracy—namely, acting as a bodyguard and personal driver for Osama bin Laden, transporting weapons used by al Qaeda members, accompanying bin Laden to al Qaeda training camps, and receiving weapons training at those camps.

Hamdan filed a habeas corpus petition in which he raised two arguments: First, conspiracy was not a war crime; and second, the rules governing military commission were so unfair to the accused that they violated both American and international law. The case went to the United States Supreme Court where, in *Hamdan v. Rumsfeld*, 548 U.S. 557 (2006), a majority of justices concluded that it would be unlawful to try Hamdan before a military commission. Justice John Paul Stevens's opinion commanded only four votes. Justice Anthony Kennedy's concurring opinion, which provided the required fifth vote, was based on narrower legal grounds.

After reviewing the history and purpose of military commissions, Justice Stevens concluded that they were appropriate only when the alleged offense took place within the theater of war and while the war was in progress; the accused could not be tried in ordinary military or civilian courts, and the offense was recognized as a war crime. In Hamdan's case, most of the alleged offenses took place before the September 11 attacks, the U.S. government had waited for years to try him, and he was currently far from the theater of battle with al Qaeda. Justice Stevens also concluded that the international community did not recognize conspiracy as a war crime.

Turning to the commission's rules, Justice Stevens observed that "in undertaking to try Hamdan and subject him to criminal punishment, the Executive is bound to comply with the Rule of Law that prevails in this jurisdiction." He concluded that the rules fell short of the standards laid down by federal law and by the Geneva Conventions, which were part of the "law of war" and therefore incorporated into the federal Uniform Code of Military Justice (UCMJ). For example, the accused could be excluded from the hearing and refused access to the evidence against him, hearsay

to preventing terrorist acts. Besides, the possibility of the death penalty does not deter a person who is willing to become a martyr to his cause. In addition, the purpose of a criminal trial is to

evidence—statements made by someone who could not be asked about them in court—was admissible, and testimony obtained through coercion was admissible as well.

Justice Anthony Kennedy agreed that the rules governing the Bush military commissions fell short of the standards laid down by the Geneva Conventions and the UCMJ. Based on that conclusion, he found it unnecessary to consider whether conspiracy was a war crime.

In one dissenting opinion, Justice Antonin Scalia maintained that the Detainee Treatment Act of 2005 barred federal courts from even hearing a habeas corpus petition filed by a Guantanamo detainee. He pointed out that the act created an appeal procedure that Hamdan could resort to if and when a commission found him guilty of war crimes.

Another dissenter, Justice Clarence Thomas, argued that courts should refrain from second-guessing the president's decisions with respect to war. Even if the Court decided the merits of this case, he argued that the Bush military commissions were lawful under the 2001 Authorization for the Use of Force, as well as the UCMJ. He also argued that conspiracy was a war crime, and had been considered one in the past. Justice Thomas observed that the law of war evolved as warfare changed, and that our response to a "new form of warfare" waged by international terrorists should not be limited by rules developed in the context of conventional wars. He went on to argue that it no longer made sense to require American troops to catch terrorists red-handed in the midst of a battle before they could be tried before a military commission. Justice Thomas also contended that *Johnson v. Eisentrager*, 1950, barred a prisoner from going to court to enforce his rights under the Geneva Conventions, and questioned whether members of al Qaeda even qualified for protection under those conventions.

The Court's ruling did not result in Hamdan's release. In 2006, Congress passed the Military Commissions Act, which drew up new procedures for military trials. Hamdan insisted that in spite of those procedures, it would still be unconstitutional to try him before a commission. In July 2008, however, a federal judge in Washington, D.C., ruled that Hamdan could not challenge the constitutionality of a military trial until after it was over. Shortly after the court's ruling, the Defense Department put Hamdan on trial before a commission sitting at Guantanamo Bay, Cuba.

decide whether an individual is guilty or innocent, not to evaluate and react to threats to national security. For that reason, the 9/11 Commission concluded that the successful prosecution of those responsible for the first World Trade Center bombings was a setback in the fight against terrorism. It explained:

> An unfortunate consequence to this superb investigative and prosecutorial effort was that it created an impression that the law enforcement system was well-equipped to cope with

The Military Commissions Act of 2006

After the Supreme Court decided *Hamdan v. Rumsfeld* (2006), Congress passed the Military Commissions Act (MCA) (Public Act 109–366). The act addressed many of the issues raised by *Hamdan* along with several other issues that were raised by lawsuits over anti-terrorism measures.

Section 3 of the MCA added a new chapter of the United States Code (10 U.S.C. §§948a-950w) that defines the procedures governing military commissions. Only non-citizens who meet the act's definition of "unlawful enemy combatant" can be tried by a commission. The act contains a number of provisions that safeguard the rights of the accused, who has many of the same rights in a military commission trial as he would have in a criminal trial. For example, the accused is presumed innocent; his guilt must be proved beyond a reasonable doubt; and he has the right to see and respond to the evidence against him, present evidence on his own behalf, and to be present at his trial. On the other hand, the accused is not entitled to a jury trial; and statements obtained through coercion can be admitted, along with hearsay evidence—that is, statements made by a person who cannot be asked about them in court. In most cases, a less-than-unanimous vote can convict. Also, the judge can restrict the accused person's right to see classified evidence against him.

The act also defines 28 "offenses that have traditionally been triable by military commissions." The list includes conspiracy, a charge that four of the eight justices who decided *Hamdan* had concluded was not a war crime.

Congress addressed several other issues that had been raised in detainees' lawsuits. Section 5(a) of the MCA bars a prisoner from relying on the Geneva

terrorism. Neither President Clinton, his principal advisers, the Congress, nor the news media felt prompted, until later, to press the question of whether the procedures that put the Blind Sheikh [Omar Abdel-Rahman] and Ramzi Yousef behind bars would protect Americans against the new virus of which these individuals were the first symptoms.[6]

Furthermore, the rules that govern criminal trials are inappropriate for dealing with terrorists. First of all, the standard of

Conventions as a source of rights. Section 6(a) provides that no person in United States custody, regardless of where he is confined, may be subject to "cruel, inhuman, or degrading" treatment. Section 6(e) strips federal courts of jurisdiction over habeas corpus petitions by non-citizen enemy combatants. A federal appeals court applied that section and barred detainees' petitions in *Boumediene v. Bush*, 476 F.3d 981 (D.C. Cir. 2007). The Supreme Court has agreed to review that decision.

The case of David Hicks, an Australian citizen, intensified the debate over military commissions. In March 2007, Hicks pled guilty to providing material support to al Qaeda and was released from Guantanamo to serve nine months in prison in his own country. According to Professor John Yoo, who supports military commissions, Hicks's case proved that the system worked. Yoo said, "One of the purposes of the military commissions was to provide a forum where the government and Al Qaeda terrorists could reach plea bargains that would allow our intelligence agencies to win their cooperation."*

Critics of military justice, however, view this case as further evidence that the system is unfair. They contend that Hicks was released because he gave prosecutors the information they wanted, which is the only way out of Guantanamo. Critics added that the government bought Hicks's silence: In order to gain his release, Hicks withdrew allegations that he had been tortured, and also promised not to speak to reporters for a year.

* Adam Liptak, "New Justice System is a Work in Progress," *New York Times*, March 29, 2007.

guilt—proof beyond a reasonable doubt—might be too high for the government to meet. Intelligence agencies must act on the basis of uncertain evidence, sometimes even on a hunch. If they are forced to work under the same restrictions as the police, they might not be able to stop terrorists from attacking. Bradford Berenson observes, "At the point of apprehension, we may not know what a terrorist is planning [and] his plans may not yet have ripened into prosecutable crimes."[7]

The rules of criminal procedure can keep important evidence from being introduced. One example is the hearsay rule, which prevents statements by non-witnesses from being used as evidence. Ruth Wedgwood, now a professor at the Johns Hopkins School of Advanced International Studies, provides an example: "[Osama] bin Laden's telephone call to his mother, telling her that 'something big' was imminent, could not be entered into evidence if the source of information was his mother's best friend."[8] Another example is the exclusionary rule, which bars the use of evidence gathered in violation of the Constitution. For example, items seized from a suspect's home by police who searched the home without a warrant cannot be used in court against the suspect. Rules such as these make it more likely that terrorists will be set free, only to stage more attacks. Bradford Berenson offers this hypothetical situation:

> [I]f Mohammed Atta had been apprehended on Sept. 10, 2001, the military could not have taken custody of him and interrogated him. And absent the ability to charge him with an ordinary crime under the U.S. Code, even the civilian authorities could not have held him for long. The only option would have been for the police to arrest him and give him a Miranda warning and a lawyer. No pressure could have been exerted to extract intelligence that might have prevented the next day's attacks, and he would have been free to alert his confederates who were still at large planning those attacks.[9]

In all likelihood, the government's evidence against accused terrorists would include military secrets, such as which terrorist cells have been infiltrated. Even the disclosure of seemingly harmless information can be damaging. During the trial of those responsible for bombing the U.S. embassies in Kenya and Tanzania, it was revealed that American intelligence had intercepted Osama bin Laden's satellite phone conversations. After that, bin Laden stopped using his satellite phone, and the United States lost track of him.

Terrorism trials also can be turned into a media circus. During the legal proceedings against him, accused terrorist Zacarias Moussaoui sometimes acted as his own lawyer and delivered long, rambling speeches that the media reported. Even worse, accused terrorists might use their trials to incite their supporters.

Finally, criminal trials are expensive and time consuming. The two trials that arose out of the 1993 World Trade Center bombing lasted for months and involved hundreds of witnesses and a vast amount of evidence. Elaborate precautions had to be taken to keep terrorists from intimidating or retaliating against the judge and jury. As retired federal judge Michael B. Mukasey (who later served as U.S. Attorney General) pointed out, "Despite the growing threat from al Qaeda and its affiliates . . . criminal prosecutions have yielded about three dozen convictions, and even those have strained the financial and security resources of the federal courts near to the limit."[10]

Military justice is a recognized means of dealing with war criminals.

Military commissions are a long-established means of dealing with war criminals. During the Revolutionary War, an ancestor of today's military commission tried British Major John Andre for spying. The first true military commission was established by General Winfield Scott during the Mexican War because there were no functioning courts in occupied Mexican territory. Then, during the Civil War, the Union Army created a commission to try war criminals, soldiers who broke military rules, and ordinary criminals found in war zones. The United States also used commissions during World War II to try German and Japanese war criminals. The most famous World War II–era commission tried eight Nazi saboteurs who were caught inside the United

Can Civilian Courts Try Terror Suspects?
United States v. Moussaoui

Advocates of military justice believe that the case of United States v. Moussaoui shows why criminal trials are not appropriate for accused terrorists. The case began in August 2001 when Zacarias Moussaoui, a French citizen, raised the suspicions of his instructors at a Minnesota flight school when he expressed an interest in flying jumbo jets and in simulating a flight from London to New York. The instructors alerted the FBI, which detained Moussaoui on immigration charges.

After the September 11 attacks, investigators found evidence that linked Moussaoui to the 19 hijackers. At first, federal authorities suggested that he was the "twentieth hijacker" who never made it aboard United Airlines Flight 93, which crashed in Pennsylvania. Moussaoui denied involvement in September 11, even though he admitted to belonging to al Qaeda. Nevertheless, a federal grand jury in Virginia indicted him on six counts of conspiring with the September 11 hijackers. Four counts carried the death penalty.

Moussaoui's trial became bogged down when the defense team demanded access to Ramzi bin al-Shibh, an al Qaeda figure who allegedly helped plan the September 11 attacks and whose testimony might clear Moussaoui of any role in the hijacking conspiracy. The defense lawyers argued that without bin al-Shibh's testimony, Moussaoui could not get a fair trial as guaranteed by the Sixth Amendment.

The government argued that in cases like this one, national security overrode the accused person's right to obtain favorable testimony. It pointed out that al-Shibh had been captured overseas and was being held as an enemy combatant, and contended that making him available would interfere with his interrogation and hamper efforts to learn about future al Qaeda attacks.

John Yoo, a law professor at the University of California, Berkeley, warned that a ruling in Moussaoui's favor could cripple future terrorism cases: "Like Moussaoui,

States. The Supreme Court upheld military trials for these men in *Ex Parte Quirin* (1942).

Supporters of military commissions reject the charge that they are "kangaroo courts" in which the outcome is known in advance. The Military Commissions Act of 2006[11] provides the

---

[accused terrorists] will call for access to every al Qaeda terrorist in U.S. custody somewhere in the world. It will be terrorism graymail, and the government will be very vulnerable to it."*

After the government refused to produce bin al-Shibh, Moussaoui's lawyers asked the judge to penalize the government for violating their client's rights. The judge found that the government had acted improperly and, in addition, that Moussaoui was a "remote or minor participant" in al Qaeda's plans. She stopped short of dismissing the charges against Moussaoui. Instead, she barred the government from seeking the death penalty or telling the jury that Moussaoui had any involvement in, or knowledge of, the September 11 attacks.

The judge's ruling presented the government with a difficult decision. If it appealed, it faced the possibility of an unfavorable ruling that would leave it with a much weaker case. On the other hand, if it dropped criminal charges and tried Moussaoui before a military commission, civil liberties groups would accuse it of "forum shopping"—looking for the court most likely to hand down a favorable judgment. And this could leave the public with the impression that the government never had a strong case. Faced with these alternatives, the government chose to appeal. After an 18-month-long legal battle, which went to the Supreme Court, Moussaoui was given access to summaries of interrogations of al Qaeda witnesses but was not allowed to call those witnesses into court.

On April 22, 2005, Moussaoui unexpectedly pled guilty to all charges. Nevertheless, he insisted that he had no intention of bringing about a September 11–type massacre, but instead sought to free Omar Abdel-Rahman, who was in prison for his involvement in the first World Trade Center bombing, and fly him to Afghanistan. After a jury failed to reach a unanimous verdict that he should get the death penalty, Moussaoui was sentenced to six consecutive life terms.

* Professor Yoo is quoted in Philip Shenon, "Judge Rules Out a Death Penalty for 9/11 Suspect," *New York Times*, October 4, 2003.

What Is a War Crime?

The Military Commissions Act of 2006 (MCA) (Public Law 109–366) spells out "offenses that have traditionally been triable by military commissions." Title 10, §950v(b) lists 28 offenses:

(1) *Murder of a protected person.* The class of "protected persons" includes civilians; military personnel who are sick, wounded, or detained as prisoners; and military medical or religious personnel.

(2) *Attacking civilians.*

(3) *Attacking civilian objects.* A "civilian object" is property that does not effectively contribute to the enemy's ability to fight a war.

(4) *Attacking protected property.* The class of "protected property" includes houses of worship, hospitals, schools, and places of historic or cultural importance, provided that the property is not being used for military purposes or is not otherwise a military objective.

(5) *Pillaging.* Unnecessarily taking the enemy's property for one's personal use.

(6) *Denying quarter.* Issuing a "take no prisoners" order.

(7) *Taking hostages.*

(8) *Employing poisons or similar weapons.*

(9) *Using protected persons as a shield.*

(10) *Using protected property as a shield.*

(11) *Torture.* It is defined as an "act specifically intended to inflict severe physical or mental pain or suffering … for the purpose of obtaining information or a confession, punishment, intimidation, coercion, or any reason based on discrimination of any kind." The term "severe mental pain or suffering" also includes administering substances aimed at profoundly disrupting the victim's senses or personality; threats of imminent death; and threatening to kill or inflict severe physical or mental pain or suffering on another person.

(12) *Cruel or inhuman treatment.* It is defined as "an act intended to inflict severe or serious physical or mental pain or suffering." The description of "serious," as opposed to "severe" pain or suffering includes a substantial risk of death, extreme physical pain, a burn or serious physical disfigurement, or the significant loss or impairment of a bodily function.

(13) *Intentionally causing serious bodily injury* in violation of the law of armed combat.

(14) *Mutilating or maiming.* This is defined as disfiguring a person or permanently disabling one of his or her organs.

(15) *Murder in violation of the law of war.*

(16) *Destruction of property in violation of the law of war.*

(17) *Using treachery or perfidy.* This offense involves creating in others the false impression that they are protected by the law of armed conflict, and then killing, injuring, or capturing them.

(18) *Improperly using a flag of truce.*

(19) *Improperly using a distinct emblem.*

(20) *Intentionally mistreating a dead body.*

(21) *Rape.*

(22) *Sexual assault or abuse.* Engaging in sexual conduct with a victim by using force, coercion, or threats.

(23) *Hijacking or hazarding a vessel or aircraft.* "Hijacking" means seizing the craft. "Hazarding" means endangering its safe navigation.

(24) *Terrorism.* A terrorist is a person who "intentionally kills or inflicts great bodily harm on one or more protected persons, or intentionally engages in an act that evinces a wanton disregard for human life, in a manner calculated to influence or affect the conduct of government or civilian population by intimidation or coercion, or to retaliate against government conduct."

(25) *Providing material support for terrorism.* "Material support or resources" means any property or service, including money or securities, financial services, lodging, training, expert advice or assistance, safe houses, false documents or identification, communications equipment, facilities, weapons, lethal substances, explosives, personnel, or transportation. Medicine and religious materials are not considered "material support."

(26) *Wrongfully aiding the enemy.* This offense can be committed only by those who owe allegiance to the United States. It requires that the offender knowingly and intentionally aid an enemy or one of its allies.

(27) *Spying.*

(28) *Conspiracy* to commit one or more offenses against the law of armed conflict.

Other provisions apply traditional principles of criminal law to the law of armed conflict. Title 10, Section 950q defines as a "principal" the person who actually

(continues)

(continued)

commits the offense. It also provides that a commanding officer who knew or who had reason to know that an offense would be committed, but failed to take action to stop it, is punishable as a principal. Section 950r provides that an accessory after the fact—someone who "receives, comforts, or assists the offender" in order to keep him from being caught and punished—can be tried by a military commission. Section 950t defines an attempt to commit a war crime as a war crime in its own right. Section 950u states that a person who "solicits or advises another" to commit a crime is liable to be tried by a military commission if the person who was solicited actually commits that offense.

accused with a number of safeguards, including the presumption of innocence and the right to be present at the trial, see and respond to the evidence against him, and offer evidence on his own behalf. A death sentence requires a unanimous vote, and a guilty verdict is reviewable by a military appeals panel and a federal appeals court.

It has also been suggested that military trials are fairer because judges are likely to make their judgment based on the facts alone. Robert Bork, a former federal appeals court judge, explains, "Military judges tend to be more scrupulous in weighing evidence, in resisting emotional appeals, and in respecting the plain import of the laws. There are no Lance Itos or Johnnie Cochrans in military trials."[12] Nor do military courts automatically convict. At the Nuremberg trials, for example, the judges found some Nazi leaders not guilty and gave others lighter sentences.

Summary

The president of the United States, as commander in chief of the armed forces, is entitled to considerable leeway in waging war, including the treatment of captured enemy fighters. The current war on terror is no exception. Both the law of armed conflict and national security considerations justify President Bush's decision to detain hundreds of fighters as unlawful combatants. The same considerations justify his use of military commissions instead of civilian courts to try non-citizens who are accused of war crimes. Because of restrictive rules of evidence and the requirement of proof beyond a reasonable doubt, civilian trials pose too great a risk that accused terrorists will go free; and such trials raise the possibility that sensitive information about U.S. counterterrorism activities will be disclosed. The use of commissions has long been recognized by international law. They provide swift justice and, at the same time, fairness to the accused.

The War on Terror Violates Human Rights

Even during wartime, presidential power is not absolute. William Rehnquist, the former chief justice of the U.S. Supreme Court, observed, "The laws will thus not be silent in times of war, but they will speak with a somewhat different voice."[1] Court decisions from past conflicts suggest that there is a limit somewhere. Critics believe that President Bush's indefinite detention of captured enemy fighters and his creation of military commissions to try war criminals went beyond that limit. Even if those measures were acceptable in past wars, some of them are contrary to modern notions of fairness and violate internationally recognized standards of human rights.

The fight against terrorism is not a "war."
Some members of the legal community take issue with President Bush's decision to assume the wartime powers of Abraham

Rasul v. Bush and Its Aftermath: The Case of the Guantanamo Detainees

After the invasion of Afghanistan, the United States military took custody of hundreds of Taliban and al Qaeda fighters at the Guantanamo Bay Naval Base in Cuba. Human rights groups began a lengthy—and still ongoing—legal battle over whether the detainees should be detained at Guantanamo.

Shortly after Guantanamo opened, lawyers filed habeas corpus petitions on behalf of a number of detainees, arguing that they were not enemy combatants and demanding an opportunity to raise the issue in court. The lower courts dismissed the petitions because *Johnson v. Eisentrager*, 339 U.S. 763 (1950), held that non-citizens held outside the United States were not protected by the Bill of Rights. They concluded that the logic of the *Eisentrager* decision applied to the Guantanamo detainees as well: Even though the United States had occupied Guantanamo for more than 100 years, it was still part of Cuba and the U.S. military was only leasing it. In *Rasul v. Bush*, 542 U.S. 466 (2004), however, the Supreme Court held that the federal habeas corpus law gave the courts the authority to hear the detainees' habeas corpus petitions. The vote was 6 to 3.

Justice John Paul Stevens wrote the majority opinion. He found important differences between the detainees in this case and the prisoners in *Eisentrager*. Most notably, the Guantanamo detainees were not citizens of countries at war with the United States and they never had an opportunity to contest their status. The *Rasul* court decision did not free the detainees. Instead, it sent the case back to the district court to determine the detainees' status. Meanwhile, Congress reacted to the decision by passing the Detainee Treatment Act of 2005 (DTA) (Public Law 109-148), which attempted to strip courts of their jurisdiction to hear Guantanamo detainees' habeas corpus petitions. In place of a court hearing, the Defense Department created Combatant Status Review Tribunals (CSRTs) to decide whether detainees should be released.

In *Hamdan v. Rumsfeld*, 548 U.S. 557 (2006), the Supreme Court held that the DTA did not strip federal courts of jurisdiction over habeas corpus cases that were *already pending* when the act became law. *Hamdan* did not free the detainees, who were again forced to start over in the district court. In the meantime, Congress passed the Military Commissions Act of 2006 (MCA) (Public Law 109-366), Section 7 of which barred federal courts from hearing the detainees' habeas

(continues)

(continued)

corpus petitions, no matter when they were filed. In that legal environment, the district court considered the detainees' petitions. Two judges came to opposite conclusions as to whether that court could hear their petition. The U.S. Court of Appeals for the District of Columbia took up the cases together on appeal and, in *Boumediene v. Bush*, 476 F.3d 981 (D.C. Cir. 2007), rejected all of the detainees' petitions. The 2-to-1 majority concluded that the detainees' right to file a habeas corpus petition was based strictly on federal law, and that one of the Congress's primary goals in passing the MCA was to overrule *Hamdan* and keep detainees' petitions out of the federal courts.

In June 2007, the Supreme Court reversed its original decision not to hear the detainees' appeal in *Boumediene*—something the justices rarely do. A year later, in *Boumediene v. Bush*, 553 U.S. ___ (2008), a 5-to-4 majority sided with the detainees. The Court ordered the government to give the detainees a habeas corpus hearing in a district court where a federal judge could conduct a meaningful review of both the government's reason for detaining them and whether it had the power to do so. In his majority opinion, Justice Anthony Kennedy first concluded that the right of habeas corpus applied to the detainees. Given the stakes involved in this case—once declared an enemy combatant, a person could spend a generation or more in prison—he rejected formalistic distinctions such as the fact that Guan-

Lincoln during the Civil War or Franklin D. Roosevelt during World War II. Anne-Marie Slaughter, the dean of Princeton University's Woodrow Wilson School of Public and International Affairs, questions whether the president's claim to broad wartime power is appropriate. She wrote: "The insistence that we are 'at war' also justifies extraordinary measures that would be unthinkable in ordinary time. In fact, the size and scale of our campaign in Afghanistan is much closer to our military campaigns in Kosovo, Bosnia, or Somalia—all specific and limited 'missions.'"[2]

Many experts believe that the fight against terror is really a large-scale police operation that will be won through international cooperation and painstaking investigative work, not

tanamo was officially on Cuban soil and that the detainees were non-citizens. Justice Kennedy next concluded that the DTA's review procedure was deficient, and thus amounted to an unconstitutional suspension of the right of habeas corpus. For example, the procedure gave a detainee no right to a lawyer and no right to see the evidence against him; and the government was free to use hearsay evidence, which was extremely difficult to challenge. Given the national security considerations involved in this case, Justice Kennedy acknowledged that it might be necessary to have all the detainees' petitions heard in the same court and to give judges discretion to prevent the disclosure of sources and intelligence-gathering methods. Beyond that, he did not lay down any ground rules for how the hearings should be conducted.

There were two dissenting opinions. Chief Justice John Roberts argued that the decision would shift even more control over foreign policy from elected officials to unelected and politically unaccountable judges, and that the DTA's review procedure was an adequate substitute for a habeas corpus hearing and therefore constitutional. Justice Antonin Scalia warned that the majority's decision would result in the death of more Americans at the hands of future terrorists.

At the time the Supreme Court decided *Boumediene*, there were an estimated 200 habeas corpus petitions pending in the court system. Legal experts believe that it will take months to rule on all of those petitions.

through military action. Sir Michael Howard prefers the British approach of treating terrorism as an "emergency," not a war. During an emergency, he explained, "the police and intelligence services were provided with exceptional powers and were reinforced where necessary by the armed forces, but they continued to operate within a peacetime framework of civilian authority."[3]

America's treatment of the enemy raises questions.

Even assuming that the United States is at war, some believe that President Bush went beyond the limits of his constitutional powers as commander in chief of the armed forces. For example, critics maintain that the president had no legal basis for refusing to hold hearings on whether the Guantanamo detainees are unlawful combatants or for denying them prisoner-of-war status and the protection that goes with it.

Some experts believe that the *Ex Parte Quirin* decision—which the Bush administration relies on as the authority for treating members of al Qaeda as unlawful combatants—misinterpreted international law. Although the law of armed combat requires a fighter to wear "fixed and distinctive emblems" and "carry arms openly," critics argue that failure to do so does not automatically make a fighter an unlawful combatant. Diane Orentlicher and Robert Goldman, law professors at American University, explain, "At the time *Quirin* was rendered, a combatant who failed to distinguish himself as required by customary law did not thereby violate the laws of war, although his specific hostile acts may have."[4]

According to the U.S. military, no more than 10 percent of the Guantanamo detainees will be charged with war crimes. Mark Denbeaux, a professor at Seton Hall University, and his son, Joshua, a lawyer, examined the Defense Department's files and concluded that most of the detainees should not have been sent to Guantanamo in the first place. The pair found that most of the detainees had not committed any hostile acts against the United States or its allies; that only 8 percent were al Qaeda fighters and most of the rest were merely affiliated with suspected terrorist groups; and that 86 percent were arrested by either Pakistan or the Northern Alliance and turned over to the U.S. military, which was offering bounties at the time.[5]

Critics also accuse the Bush administration of two other violations of the Geneva Conventions. The first was refusing to convene a "competent tribunal" to determine the status of enemy fighters. The second was refusing to treat those fighters as prisoners of war pending a decision by the tribunal. Until the Supreme Court handed down its ruling in *Rasul*, the Pentagon simply classified all of the Guantanamo detainees as unlawful combatants and insisted that its decision was final. Some legal experts also point out that the term "unlawful combatants" appears nowhere in the Geneva Conventions. They accuse the Bush administration of having invented a category of second-class military prisoners.

Even if the Constitution gives the president final authority to decide who is an unlawful combatant, his doing so could result in a miscarriage of justice. Former Vice President Al Gore contended, "Now if the President makes a mistake, or is given faulty information by somebody working for him, and locks up the wrong person, then it's almost impossible for that person to prove his innocence—because he can't talk to a lawyer or his family or anyone else and he doesn't even have the right to know what specific crime he is accused of committing."[6] Critics argue that the Bush administration's treatment of enemy fighters is contrary to American policy in past conflicts. In both the Vietnam War and the 1991 Gulf War, the U.S. military followed the Geneva Conventions and convened tribunals to determine the status of captured enemy fighters. Military regulations establish specific procedures for such tribunals.

Finally, human rights groups accuse the administration of acting as a law unto itself. They contend that the military located a prison at Guantanamo because government lawyers believed that it was outside the jurisdiction of American courts.

Military justice is unfair.

Hamdan v. Rumsfeld, 2006, concluded that the rules governing President Bush's military commissions fell short of both the Geneva Conventions and the federal Uniform Code of Military Justice (UCMJ). Even though Congress responded to the court's objections by passing the Military Commissions Act of 2006 (MCA), civil liberties groups still consider military justice unfair. First of all, they argue that an overly broad category of individuals can be tried before commissions. The MCA contains a two-part definition of "unlawful enemy combatant." The first part of that definition is relatively specific: "a person who has engaged in hostilities or who has purposefully and materially supported hostilities against the United States or its co-belligerents who is not a lawful enemy combatant (including a person who is part of the Taliban, al Qaeda, or associated forces)."[7] The second part of the definition, however, is not specific. It defines an enemy combatant as "a person who, before, on, or after the date of the enactment of the Military Commissions Act of 2006, has been determined to be an unlawful enemy combatant by a Combatant Status Review Tribunal or another competent tribunal."[8]

Habeas Corpus

Habeas corpus, Latin for "you may have the body," is a writ, or court order. A writ of habeas corpus orders a person who is responsible for a person's detention—typically, a prison warden—to bring the prisoner into court so that a judge may decide whether that person is being lawfully detained. It has been called the "Great Writ" because it acts as a judicial check on executive authority to detain individuals. In *Fay v. Noia*, 372 U.S. 391, 402 (1963), U.S. Supreme Court Justice William Brennan said of habeas corpus, "Its root principle is that in a civilized society, government must always be accountable to the judiciary for a man's imprisonment: If the imprisonment cannot be shown to conform with the fundamental requirements of law, the individual is entitled to his immediate release."

The historical roots of habeas corpus are not clear, but Section 39 of the Magna Carta (1215) is often cited as its source. That section states, "No free man shall be seized, or imprisoned, or disseised, or outlawed, or exiled, or injured in any way, nor will we enter on him or send against him except by the lawful judgment of his peers, or by the law of the land."

The essential elements of the writ of habeas corpus were spelled out by England's Parliament in the Habeas Corpus Act of 1679. It was part of the English common law that the United States adopted after independence, and was guaranteed by most early state constitutions. People in the colonies had held habeas

Opponents of military commissions also argue that people other than accused war criminals may find themselves before a military commission. A task force of leading American lawyers found "it is not clear that membership, alone, in al Qaeda or harboring terrorists violates the law of war," and added, "not all acts of international terrorism are necessarily violations of the law of war."[9]

Even though the MCA offers the accused more protection than the commissions originally created by President Bush, serious questions of fairness persist. The judges and the lawyers for both sides are military officers who belong to the same chain of command, raising the possibility of pressure from higher-ups

corpus in high regard, and the Crown's refusal to issue writs was one of the grievances that led to the American Revolution. The U.S. Constitution specifically mentions habeas corpus. The so-called Suspension Clause, Article I, Section 9, Clause 2, states: "The Privilege of the Writ of Habeas Corpus shall not be suspended, unless when in Cases of Rebellion or Invasion the public Safety may require it." The Judiciary Act of 1789, enacted by the First Congress, gave federal courts authority to issue writs of habeas corpus.

Habeas corpus is used primarily to challenge a criminal conviction on the grounds that the convicted person has not received a fair trial. However, it has also been used to challenge one's confinement in a mental institution, quarantine for health reasons, and has even been used in disputes over child custody. Habeas corpus also has been used by people who were detained by the United States during the fight against terrorism.

A habeas corpus proceeding is civil in nature; in other words, it tests only whether a prisoner was given due process, not whether the person is guilty or innocent. There is no time limit on filing a petition because the right of personal freedom from illegal restraint never lapses. Furthermore, an unsuccessful habeas corpus petition does not bar a person from filing another petition later, although Congress and the courts have limited the number of petitions that some convicted criminals may file. Finally, because prisoners are often held incommunicado, the law allows a relative or lawyer to file a petition as the prisoner's "next friend."

Who Is an "Enemy Combatant"? *Al-Marri v. Wright*

In *Hamdi v. Rumsfeld*, 2004, Justice Sandra Day O'Connor left to the lower courts the task of defining who was an "enemy combatant." That definition became a central issue in Ali al-Marri's effort to get out of military custody.

Al-Marri, a citizen of Qatar, came to the United States in September 2001 to study for a master's degree. He was originally taken into custody as a material witness who had important information about the September 11 attacks, then charged with credit card and identity fraud, and eventually declared an enemy combatant and moved to a military prison.

Al-Marri filed a habeas corpus petition challenging his detention. The government argued that al-Marri belonged in military custody because he had trained at an al Qaeda camp, had been introduced to Osama bin Laden himself, and had been sent to the United States as a "sleeper agent" to disrupt computers used for the U.S. financial system. Al-Marri offered no evidence in rebuttal. A federal district court in South Carolina ruled in the government's favor but in *Al-Marri v. Wright*, 487 F.3d 160 (4th Cir. 2007), a three-judge panel of the U.S. Court of Appeals for the Fourth Circuit concluded that al-Marri was being improperly detained.

The vote was 2 to 1. Writing for the majority, Judge Diana Gribbon Motz concluded that alleged criminal activity in association with a terrorist organization did not, by itself, make al-Marri an unlawful enemy combatant. She found this case analogous to *Ex Parte Milligan*, 1866, in which the Supreme Court concluded that Lambdin Milligan could not be tried by a military commission because he had neither fought alongside the Confederates nor taken orders

to reach a guilty verdict. Commissions have broad leeway in deciding what evidence to consider, including hearsay evidence and testimony obtained through coercion. At the trial, the judge can restrict the accused person's right to see classified evidence against him. Unless the accused faces the death penalty, a guilty verdict does not require a unanimous vote. Finally, even though the act provides for review by civilian

from them. She stressed, however, that the court's decision did not require the government to set al-Marri free. It could instead charge him with crimes, as it did with Zacarias Moussaoui and attempted "shoe bomber" Richard Reid; hold him as a material witness; or expel him from the country. Judge Motz also expressed concern that the government had moved al-Marri to military custody for the purpose of interrogating him—even though Justice O'Connor had stated in *Hamdi* that "indefinite detention for the purpose of interrogation is not authorized." There was basis for Judge Motz's concern. In his book *Never Again*, former Attorney General John Ashcroft called al-Marri a "hard case" who refused to provide the government with information about al Qaeda in exchange for a lighter sentence.

The government asked all nine judges on the Fourth Circuit to reconsider this case. The result was *Al-Marri v. Pucciarelli*, No. 06-7427 (U.S. Ct. App., 4th Cir., July 15, 2008), in which there were seven different opinions. Even though no single opinion commanded a majority, five judges concluded that if the government's allegations against al-Marri were true, then the 2001 authorization for the use of military force against those responsible for the September 11 attacks gave the government power to detain him as an enemy combatant. However, Judge William Traxler, one of the five who upheld al-Marri's detention, also concluded that the government could not detain al-Marri simply on the basis of a sworn statement from a defense intelligence official. He did not, however, lay down any ground rules for such a hearing. Even though the appeals court sent the case back to the district court to determine whether al-Marri is an unlawful enemy combatant, legal experts believe that it will ultimately come before the Supreme Court.

courts, critics believe that the scope of review is too limited to challenge the commission procedures themselves. Given the stakes involved, the risk of convicting an innocent person is unacceptably high.

In any event, opponents believe that military commissions are inherently unfair. Diane Orentlicher and Robert Goldman explain, "Human rights instruments binding on the United

States mandate that criminal defendants, whatever their offenses, be tried by independent and impartial courts that afford generally recognized due process guarantees. By their very nature, military commissions do not satisfy this basic test."[10]

Mistreatment of enemy fighters hurts America's image.

In 2004, the world saw graphic photographs that depicted American soldiers abusing Iraqi prisoners at Abu Ghraib prison in Baghdad. The news media have also reported that interrogators from the Central Intelligence Agency (CIA) had engaged in "waterboarding," or simulated drowning, of prisoners, as well as other abusive practices; maintained a network of secret prisons; and handed prisoners over to foreign countries that use torture to extract information. But the number-one symbol of America's lack of respect for human rights remains the military prison at Guantanamo Bay.

Even though the military has created Combatant Status Review Tribunals (CSRTs) to determine detainees' status, Mark and Joshua Denbeaux concluded, after examining the records of hundreds of cases, that the tribunals were a sham.[11] They found that the government's case typically consisted entirely of a summary of the evidence against the detainee. What followed was a classic Catch-22. The tribunal accepted the summary as authoritative evidence, but at the same time refused to give the detainee a meaningful opportunity to challenge that evidence—for example, by calling witnesses—or even to see evidence that the military labeled "classified." In all 102 cases for which the Denbeaux team had a full record, the CSRT unanimously ruled that the detainee was an enemy combatant. Military authorities at Guantanamo also have been accused of inconsistency. A December 2006 *New York Times* story reported that "some detainees have been held for years, while other detainees against whom there seemed to be stronger evidence of militant activities have been released under secret agreements between the U.S. and their home governments."[12]

Observers warn that the Bush administration's treatment of the detainees has damaged America's reputation abroad. Some accuse the administration of hypocrisy: It condemns other countries for trying political opponents before military commissions, but does the same to alleged terrorists. Others fear that because America violates human rights standards in the name of fighting terrorism, there will be a worldwide "race to the bottom." International lawyer John Whitbeck explains:

> Not surprisingly, since September 11, virtually every recognized state confronting an insurgency or separatist movement has eagerly jumped on the "war on terrorism" bandwagon, branding its domestic opponents (if it had not already done so) "terrorists" and, at least implicitly, taking the position that, since no one dares to criticize the United States for doing whatever it deems necessary in its "war on terrorism," no one should criticize whatever they now do to suppress their own "terrorists."[13]

The actions of the United States also create the risk that other countries will retaliate against Americans abroad, particularly those serving in the armed forces. Al Gore warns, "If we don't provide [POW treatment to detainees], how can we expect American soldiers captured overseas to be treated with equal respect? We owe this to our sons and daughters who fight to defend freedom in Iraq, in Afghanistan, and elsewhere in the world."[14] Furthermore, recognizing a "terrorism exception" to the rule of law could lead to a gradual erosion of the civil liberties enjoyed by Americans. Author and journalist Edwin Dobb argues, "civil rights lose their legitimacy, their claim on our conscience, as soon as any one person is excluded from their protection."[15]

There are alternatives to military justice.

Human rights groups have criticized the Bush administration
for its announced intention to hold the Guantanamo detainees until the conflict with al Qaeda is over. Had the Supreme
Court not ruled in the detainees' favor in *Rasul*, many of them
could have been detained for the rest of their lives—even if
they were wholly innocent of wrongdoing. Ronald Dworkin,
a legal philosopher who teaches at New York University, has
suggested a two-month time limit for deciding whether to
classify a detainee as a prisoner of war or a potential war
criminal, and recommends releasing a prisoner of war after
three years, by which time any intelligence he might offer has
become stale.

Legal experts also have suggested alternatives to military
commissions. One such alternative is an international tribunal, similar to that used at Nuremberg, to try leading al Qaeda
figures. Some suggest inviting judges from Islamic countries
to take part so the trials will not be seen as Western persecu-
tion of Muslims. Another proposal is that Congress create special "national security courts" with a corps of specially trained
judges, prosecutors, and defense lawyers. Those courts would
have the power to detain suspected terrorists in cases while an
investigation in underway. Yet another suggestion, offered by
a panel of New York City lawyers, is to try accused war criminals by court-martial rather than before a commission. In his
opinion in *Hamdan*, Justice John Paul Stevens seemed to agree.
He wrote:

> The military commission was not born of a desire to dis-
> pense a more summary form of justice than is afforded
> by courts-martial; it developed, rather, as a tribunal of
> necessity to be employed when courts-martial lacked
> jurisdiction over either the accused or the subject mat-
> ter.... Exigency lent the commission its legitimacy, but

did not further justify the wholesale jettisoning of procedural protections. That history explains why the military commission's procedures typically have been the ones used by courts-martial.[16]

The fact that the MCA incorporated most of the rules governing courts-martial into commission procedures suggests that there was no need to create the commissions in the first place.

Finally, some believe that civilian courts can and should be used to try low-level terrorists, as well as those charged with aiding terrorist organizations by committing crimes such as money laundering. Supporters point out that civilian courts have tried criminals who have violated international law—including pirates and slave traders—since the founding of this country. In recent years, those courts have convicted John Walker Lindh, the American who fought alongside the Taliban; Richard Reid, who attempted to detonate a "shoe bomb" aboard a trans-Atlantic jet; and Jose Padilla, who was found guilty of conspiring to aid terrorists. They also maintain that there are ways to ensure security, such as keeping cameras out of the courtroom, protecting the identity of jurors and witnesses, and severely punishing those who disclose sensitive information.

Summary

Some experts dispute whether the war on terror is really a "war" and even if it is, whether the scope of the conflict justifies the president's assertion of the broad powers claimed by past wartime presidents. Critics maintain that the president has no legal authority to declare enemy fighters "unlawful combatants," detain them indefinitely, or try them before military commissions. Even if the treatment of enemy fighters is constitutional, many warn that it violates international human rights standards and tarnishes this country's reputation, especially in the Muslim world. The treatment of the Guantanamo detainees has been especially damaging. In addition, the United States' violation of international law invites other countries to commit similar violations, possibly against Americans serving in the military or traveling overseas.

New Laws Are Needed to Fight Terrorism

John Ashcroft, who was U.S. attorney general at the time of the September 11 attacks, said afterward that it is necessary to re-think the balance between liberty and safety. He wrote:

> When the founders of our country and the writers of the Constitution put all the safeguards in place, at the time of the American Revolution, a single individual might have been able to carry explosives that could damage a room or a small structure. Today, a single terrorist could do more damage than a frigate sailing through Boston Harbor might have threatened during the Revolution. Today, one man might transport catastrophic explosive capacity or evil biology or radiology and, in worse cases, combine them to threaten metropolitan areas and hundreds of thousands of lives.[1]

The terrorist threat requires new legal tools.

Military force alone cannot defeat al Qaeda, whose members dress as civilians and live among innocent citizens. The fight requires law enforcement and intelligence work, both at home and abroad. Over the years, as criminals became more sophisticated, law enforcement agencies were given new legal tools to deal with them. Al Qaeda presents threats of even greater magnitude than ordinary criminals because it intends to kill thousands of Americans. It is also difficult for law enforcement agencies to infiltrate terrorist cells. For those reasons, police and prosecutors need at least the same legal weapons to fight terrorism that they have to fight drug lords and crime syndicates. As Senator Joseph Biden argued during floor debate on the Patriot Act, "The FBI could get a wiretap to investigate the Mafia, but they could not get one to investigate terrorists. To put it bluntly, that was crazy! What's good for the mob should be good for terrorists."[2]

The Patriot Act has given authorities those weapons. For example, Section 206 allows the use of "roving wiretaps," which apply to any phone or computer a suspected terrorist might use. John Ashcroft explains why they are necessary:

> [I]n the 1980s, drug dealers developed a habit of throwing away their phones regularly. They had discovered that it often took law officers more than a week to get a new court order to operate to monitor their phone calls on a particular telephone. If the drug dealers changed to a new phone every so often, that could give them at least a week to operate without surveillance.[3]

The use of roving wiretaps has been legal in drug investigations since 1986. A related provision, Section 220 of the act, authorizes courts to issue nationwide search warrants, a law enforcement tool that is needed to keep up with terrorists who use multiple cell phones and send e-mail from Internet cafes.

President Bush speaks with lawmakers before he signs the USA PATRIOT Act into law on October 26, 2001. The Act gave law enforcement officials more authority to gather information about suspected terrorist activities.

The Patriot Act also updated the federal criminal code. It created new terrorism-related offenses such as harboring terrorists and unlawfully possessing a biological weapon. It also imposed longer prison terms on convicted terrorists, and eliminated the time limit for prosecuting crimes involving terrorism. The act also gave the Treasury Department new powers to disrupt the financing of terrorist organizations and made it easier for the Justice Department to detain and deport non-citizens who have links to terrorists.

Perhaps most importantly, the Patriot Act addressed a serious obstacle to catching terrorists—namely, the legal "wall" that separated domestic law enforcement from foreign intelligence gathering. The wall was created in the 1970s, after it was revealed that government agencies spied on thousands of political opponents, such as Dr. Martin Luther King Jr. But the

Major Provisions of the Patriot Act

After the September 11 attacks, Congress passed the "Uniting and Strengthening America by Providing Appropriate Tools Required to Intercept and Obstruct Terrorism" (Public Law 107–56). The law is referred to by its acronym, the USA PATRIOT Act, or simply the "Patriot Act." John Ashcroft, who was attorney general at the time, argued that the act brought about some long-needed changes to the law. He wrote: "The Patriot Act updated the law to counter new technologies and new threats. We no longer have to fight a digital-age battle with antique analog weapons, not to mention legal authorities left over from the era of rotary telephones."*

The act's most controversial provisions deal with government surveillance. Overall, these provisions widen the scope of searches and lessen court supervision of government agencies that monitor people. Some surveillance provisions apply to criminal investigations in general. Others apply to "foreign intelligence" investigations, which focus on the activities of agents of foreign powers—including suspected terrorists. Foreign intelligence searches are governed by the Foreign Intelligence Surveillance Act of 1978 (FISA), which imposes a lower standard for intelligence surveillance than for an investigation of ordinary criminal activity.

Major provisions of the act include the following:

Section 203. Makes it easier for law enforcement agencies to share foreign intelligence gathered in a criminal investigation.

Section 206. Permits "roving wiretaps," which apply to any phone or computer a surveillance target might use, including computers at public facilities.

Section 209. Allows the government to get a court order to seize voice mail as well as e-mail messages.

Section 213. The so-called "sneak-and-peek" provision. Allows a law enforcement agency to execute a search warrant without first notifying the person searched. The agency must show a court that notification would cause an "adverse result."

Section 215. The so-called "library provision." It authorizes court orders directing third-party holders of business records—such as financial, medical, or library records—to turn them over to the government if they are relevant to a terrorism investigation.

Section 216. Imposes clearer standards for government monitoring of Internet use. A court order is required, and the content of online communications—as opposed to e-mail addresses or URLs of Web sites—may not be monitored.

Section 218. Expands the government's power to gather foreign intelligence. To carry out surveillance, the government must show that foreign intelligence information is merely "a significant purpose," rather than "the purpose," of the search.

Section 220. Allows federal courts to issue nationwide search warrants for electronic evidence such as e-mail communications.

Section 412. Authorizes the detention of a non-citizen for up to seven days without being charged if the person is a danger to national security. Allows detention beyond the seven-day period if the person is deportable and release would endanger national security.

Section 501. Authorizes the Justice Department to offer cash rewards for information about terrorism.

Section 503. Requires persons convicted of a terrorism offense or any violent crime to provide a sample for the national DNA database.

Section 505. Authorizes the FBI to issue a "national security letter" directing a holder of business records to turn them over. The FBI must certify that the records are relevant to an ongoing terrorism investigation and that the person whose records are asked for is an "agent of a foreign power."

Section 507. Authorizes the Justice Department to obtain a court order seeking educational records relevant to a terrorism investigation.

Sections 801–803. Creates the following new crimes: attacking a mass transportation system, domestic terrorism, and harboring terrorists.

Section 804. Expands the definition of the crime of providing "material support" to terrorists.

Section 806. Authorizes the government to confiscate the foreign and domestic assets of terrorist organizations.

Sections 810–811. Increases maximum penalties for certain terror-related crimes.

Section 817. Creates the new crime of unlawful possession of a biological weapon.

In March 2006, Congress passed the USA PATRIOT Improvement and Reauthorization Act of 2005 (Public Act 109–174). The law made relatively few changes to

(continues)

(continued)
the original act, and made most of its highly controversial provisions permanent. However, the reauthorization did offer some additional protection of privacy. It amended Section 215 by requiring the government to provide a fuller explanation of why it needs to examine business records, and permits the holder of business records, such as a library, to go to court to challenge an order to produce those records. It also required the government to provide a court with a fuller explanation of why it wants to conduct a roving wiretap. In addition, the legislation provided for closer congressional oversight of some of the surveillance that the Patriot Act authorizes, such as roving wiretaps and national security letters. In some cases, the Justice Department must report to Congress on its surveillance activities.

*John Ashcroft, *Never Again: Securing America and Restoring Justice*. New York: Center Street, 2006: pp. 159–160.

wall impeded the government's investigation of terrorist activity. Prosecutor Patrick Fitzgerald, who was part of the team that prosecuted those responsible for the first World Trade Center attack, explained:

> We could talk to citizens, local police officers, other U.S. government agencies, foreign police officers—even foreign intelligence personnel, and foreign citizens. We did all those things. We could even talk to al Qaeda members—and we did. But there was one group of people we were not permitted to talk to. Who? The FBI agents across the street from us assigned to a parallel intelligence investigation of Osama bin Laden and al Qaeda. We could not learn what information they had gathered. That was "the wall."[4]

Many believe that the wall prevented authorities from stopping the September 11 attacks. In the days leading up to the attacks, the government knew that two of the hijackers, Khalid al-Mihdhar and Nawaf al-Hazmi, were in the United States but could not locate them. Had they been found, the other hijackers might have been tracked down. An FBI intelligence agent in New York who was looking for al-Mihdhar and al-Hazmi asked the bureau's criminal investigators for help in finding them. His higher-ups turned him down, telling him that criminal information could not be passed over the wall. The intelligence agent responded with the following e-mail:

> Whatever has happened to this—someday someone will die—and wall or not—the public will not understand why we were not more effective and throwing every resource we had at certain "problems."
>
> Let's hope the National Security Law Unit will stand behind their decisions then, especially since the biggest threat to us now, UBL [Osama bin Laden], is getting the most "protection."[5]

Section 203 of the Patriot Act specifically allows law enforcement and foreign intelligence personnel to share information. Many legal experts believe that this provision was not only necessary but also overdue because it makes little sense to draw fine legal distinctions between crime and terrorism when dealing with an enemy as dangerous as al Qaeda.

Critics exaggerate the dangers of anti-terrorism laws.

As a wartime measure, the Patriot Act is modest compared to those of past conflicts. It does not affect basic rights such as habeas corpus and the presumption of innocence in criminal trials, and courts continue to oversee searches carried out by law enforcement agencies. There have been some civil liberties violations under the act, but they were not systematic, as they were when, for example, President Abraham Lincoln used military commissions to punish his critics, or when the military interned Japanese Americans during World War II.

Supporters believe that the Patriot Act has been unfairly criticized. They complain that critics have focused on a handful of provisions and read them out of context to create the impression that the government has been given dangerous new powers. One example is Section 213 of the act, which allows law enforcement agencies to search a person's property without first notifying him. Critics call it the "sneak-and-peek" provision. John Ashcroft explains why these searches are necessary:

The Terrorist Surveillance Program

After the September 11 attacks, President Bush directed the National Security Agency to begin a counterterrorism program called the Terrorist Surveillance Program. The NSA, which is part of the Defense Department, is responsible for collecting and analyzing foreign communications. Even though many of the details of the TSP are secret, the government has stated that the program involves surveillance of telephone and e-mail communications in which one party lives outside the United States and the other party is believed to have links to al Qaeda.

A December 2005 story in *The New York Times*, which disclosed TSP's existence, provoked debate as to whether President Bush had broken the law. It was found that the president decided to bypass a special court that hears government requests to eavesdrop on suspected terrorists. Congress created the court in 1978 as part of the Foreign Intelligence Surveillance Act (FISA) (50 U.S.C. §§1801 and following). Congress passed FISA after it learned that government agencies had engaged in abusive surveillance, including wiretapping such prominent figures as Dr. Martin Luther King, Jr.

Because intelligence gathering is not the same as looking for evidence of a crime, FISA imposes fewer restrictions than would apply in a criminal investigation. Nevertheless, President Bush insisted that the law's requirements were too cumbersome and that it was important to take swift action to find and stop terrorists. The president also claimed that he had inherent power as commander in chief of the armed forces to monitor enemy communications in a time of war.

Imagine this scenario: Terrorists sneak a nuclear bomb into a major U.S. city and threaten to detonate it. The FBI learns that an individual has the plans in his house that describe the location and the detonation procedure for the device. The FBI searches the house without notifying the individual who lives there, and the agents discover the plan revealing the location of the nuclear device. Yet the FBI would not want the person living at the house to know that he had been searched until agents had found and disarmed the nuclear bomb. Otherwise, with one phone call, a simple signal, perhaps, the person at the

Civil liberties groups countered that the president defied the clear intent of Congress that all surveillance, even in wartime, be conducted under FISA. They contended that his surveillance program not only violated FISA, but also the Fourth Amendment to the U.S. Constitution, which prohibits unreasonable searches and seizures. The American Civil Liberties Union and a number of individuals filed suit to stop the program, but the U.S. Court of Appeals for the Sixth Circuit ruled for the government in *American Civil Liberties Union v. National Security Agency*, 493 F.3d 644 (6th Cir.). The appeals court found it unnecessary to rule on the lawfulness of the president's surveillance program because it concluded that those who challenged it failed to show that it had affected them.

The Bush administration and many public officials insisted that FISA hampered the government's ability to fight terrorists. Matters came to a head in August 2007, after the FISA court reportedly ruled that portions of the Terrorist Surveillance Program were unlawful. At the president's urging, Congress passed the Protect America Act of 2007 (Public Act 110–55), which gave the Justice Department and intelligence agencies more leeway in conducting surveillance programs. Civil liberties groups contend that the new law makes it possible for the government to monitor law-abiding Americans' telephone conversations and e-mail messages with little supervision by either the courts or Congress.

In 2008, Congress debated whether to make the provisions of the Protect America Act permanent—something President Bush insisted was necessary—and also debated whether to absolve telecom companies from legal liability for their participation in the surveillance program.

house could notify his co-conspirators to detonate the bomb before the agents would have a chance to interrupt the plan.[6]

Nor is delayed notification a new concept. Some time ago, courts recognized that there were circumstances in which the police could search first and notify the owner afterward.

Another much-criticized provision of the Patriot Act is Section 215, which permits law enforcement agencies to order a business, such as a bank, to turn over its customers' records. The nation's librarians warned that Section 215 increased the likelihood that information pertaining to a library patron would be seized without his or her knowledge. But grand juries have long had the power to issue subpoenas for evidence of criminal activity. All that Section 215 does is provide a means of gathering information in a national security investigation where no grand jury is involved. Furthermore, Section 215 specifically provides that an American citizen cannot be investigated "solely upon the basis of activities protected by the First Amendment to the Constitution."[7] In any event, the FBI has rarely used this provision, and has never asked a library to turn over patrons' borrowing records.

Another misunderstood provision is Section 216, which allows law enforcement authorities to monitor a person's online activity. Like many Patriot Act provisions, this section merely adapted existing legal concepts to new technology. For years, courts have authorized the police to use devices to record the telephone numbers of suspected criminals' incoming and outgoing calls. Section 216 allows much the same surveillance of electronic communications. Section 216 is also an example of how the Patriot Act *improved* the law. In 1986, Congress tried to legalize surveillance of electronic communications, but the law was so badly written that the police were still not sure what was permissible. Section 216 not only laid down a clear legal standard, but also gave computer users the same privacy protection as telephone users.

Anti-terrorism laws have worked.

The Patriot Act has also helped authorities prevent another terrorist attack. John Ashcroft, who credits the act with breaking up
alleged terrorist cells in Buffalo, Detroit, Portland, and Seattle,
offers the details of one Patriot Act success story:

> Prosecutors and investigators shared information in inves-
> tigating the defendants in the "Virginia Jihad" case. This
> prosecution involved members of the Dar al-Arqam Islamic
> Center, who trained for jihad ("struggle" in Arabic, though
> usually interpreted to mean "holy war") in northern Virginia.
> Eight of those individuals traveled to terrorist training camps
> in Pakistan or Afghanistan between 1999 and 2001. These
> individuals are associates of a violent Islamic extremist group
> known as Lashkar-e-Taiba, which operates in Pakistan and
> Kashmir, and has ties to al Qaeda. As a result of using infor-
> mation obtained through electronic surveillance, prosecutors
> were able to bring charges against these individuals. Six of the
> defendants pleaded guilty, and three were convicted in March
> 2004 of charges including conspiracy to levy war against the
> United States and conspiracy to provide material support to
> the Taliban. . . . In this particular case, it would have been
> much more difficult to arrest, charge, and convict these ter-
> rorists had agents and prosecutors not been able to share
> information.[8]

The Justice Department also gives credit to the Patriot Act for
the arrests of Sami al-Arian, the alleged American leader of Pal-
estinian Islamic Jihad, a terrorist group responsible for murder-
ing more than 100 people, including a young American woman
killed in Gaza; and Hemant Lekhani, an alleged arms dealer
charged with attempting to sell shoulder-fired missiles to terrorists for use against American targets such as passenger jets.

Finally, the Patriot Act has had little effect on most Americans' lives. In a July 2003 FOX News/Opinion Dynamics poll, 91

percent believed that the act had not affected their civil liberties. Average Americans are unlikely to feel the effects of post–September 11 security measures except when they go to the airport or attend a sporting event. The fact that Congress not only renewed the Patriot Act in 2006, but also left intact almost all of the original act's provisions, suggests that critics exaggerated the threat it posed to civil liberties.

Liberty is impossible without security.

Supporters of anti-terrorism measures insist that they are not overreactions to the September 11 attacks. John Ashcroft pointed out that after the attacks, authorities detained only people who were in violation of the law. In contrast, during World War II, the United States detained thousands of innocent people, including American citizens of Japanese and German descent. Ashcroft also warned Americans that his department would not tolerate vigilante activity aimed at law-abiding Arabs and Muslims.

Those who favor stronger anti-terrorism laws also emphasize that the purpose of government is not only to safeguard citizens' freedom, but also to protect their lives. They maintain that, "there is no more basic civil liberty than the right not to be blown to bits."[9] Even assuming that some laws might have gone too far, supporters of strong anti-terrorism laws insist that the alternative is worse still:

> Imagine what would happen if the war against terrorism fails. Repeated attacks would create panic, and a terrible backlash against civil liberties would ensue. As the casualty toll grew, the calls for Draconian measures would make the rather modest provisions in the Administration's anti-terrorist package pale by comparison. A long twilight struggle against terrorism that proves ineffective would chip away at the Constitution in ways Americans can scarcely imagine.[10]

The 9/11 Commission and its Recommendations

In November 2002, President Bush and Congress established the National Commission on Terrorist Attacks Upon the United States, commonly known as the 9/11 Commission. Over the year and a half that followed, it reviewed more than 2.5 million pages of documents; interviewed more than 1,200 people in 10 countries, including many top officials of the Bill Clinton and George W. Bush administrations; and held 19 days of hearings, taking public testimony from 160 witnesses.

The 9/11 Commission was headed by former New Jersey Governor Thomas Kean, a Republican, and former U.S. Representative Lee Hamilton, a Democrat. The commission was not concerned with assigning blame for the attacks. Instead, it focused on why they succeeded and what could be done to prevent future attacks.

In its report*, the commission conceded that it was impossible to reduce the risk of a terrorist attack to zero, but it did conclude that the risk could be minimized. To accomplish that goal, it made 41 recommendations, including the following:

- Identifying actual and potential terrorist sanctuaries, and developing a strategy for keeping terrorists there on the run

- Providing moral leadership in the world. That leadership includes defending Muslims against tyrants and criminals in their own countries.

- Developing economic policies that encourage development, open societies, and broader opportunities for people in Muslim countries

- Taking steps to make it harder for terrorists to travel between countries or obtain funds for their operations

- Following the Geneva Conventions' standards for the treatment of suspected terrorists held in custody

- Strengthening and expanding efforts to stop the proliferation of weapons of mass destruction, especially nuclear weapons

- Upgrading border security, including implementing an entry/exit screening system that relies on individual physical characteristics such as fingerprints

- Making broader use of "no-fly" lists at airports and screening all passengers for explosives

(continues)

(continued)

- Establishing federal standards for the issuance of documents such as driver's licenses

- Taking steps to safeguard the privacy of individuals about whom federal agencies share information

- Requiring the government to prove that new anti-terrorism powers are necessary and that there is adequate supervision of the use of those powers to ensure that privacy is protected

The commission found that even though the Cold War ended years ago, the country's national security institutions were still designed to fight it. Some of the commission's recommendations were aimed at restructuring the government to meet the threat of terrorism. They included the following:

- Establishing a National Counterterrorism Center, which would become primarily responsible for analyzing terrorist threats

- Creating a new position of director of national intelligence, who would oversee federal agencies' intelligence operations

- Refocusing the Central Intelligence Agency on gathering and analyzing information

- Transferring secret military operations, such as attempting to capture or kill Osama bin Laden, from the CIA to the Defense Department

Summary

Throughout the nation's history, it has been necessary to balance liberty and security. The al Qaeda terrorist organization, which perpetrated the worst attack on this country since World War II, intends to attack again. In light of that threat, the United States has no choice but to take measures aimed at stopping the terrorists. Even though the Patriot Act and other anti-terrorism laws expanded the government's power, they did so to a much

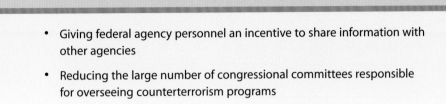

- Giving federal agency personnel an incentive to share information with other agencies

- Reducing the large number of congressional committees responsible for overseeing counterterrorism programs

- Instituting a "fast track" confirmation process for nominees to key positions so that a new president could quickly assemble his or her national security team.

- Creating a specialized national security unit within the FBI. However, the commissioners rejected the idea of creating a domestic intelligence agency similar to Britain's MI5.

Three years after the report's publication, Congress passed the Implementing Recommendations of the 9/11 Commission Act of 2007 (Public Law 110–53), which aims to carry out most of the commission's recommendations. But even before the 2007 act became law, some recommendations had already been implemented. Congress had created the Department of Homeland Security, which brought 20 federal agencies with security-related responsibilities within a single federal department; reorganized intelligence agencies and created the position of director of national intelligence; mandated tougher security requirements for driver's licenses and other identification documents; and placed new restrictions aimed at stopping the flow of money to terrorists.

* National Commission on Terrorist Attacks Upon the United States, *The 9/11 Commission Report: Final Report of the National Commission on Terrorist Attacks Upon the United States* New York: W.W. Norton & Company, 2004.

lesser extent than measures used to win past wars. Most of the Patriot Act's provisions merely took existing legal principles and adapted them to modern technology. Despite warnings that the Patriot Act would lead to abuses, it has been narrowly focused on terrorists and their supporters, and thus abuses have been uncommon. In any event, anti-terrorism laws have reduced the risk of another attack and the harsh restrictions on liberty that would almost surely follow.

Anti-terrorism Laws Are Ineffective and Dangerous

Civil liberties advocates accuse the Bush administration of fearmongering: using the threat of future terrorist attacks to pressure Congress to pass measures such as the Patriot Act and the Protect America Act of 2007,[1] which broadened the administration's power to monitor telephone and e-mail communications. They believe that lawmakers did not fully understand the extent to which these laws would affect civil liberties. They further contend that post–September 11 anti-terrorism laws concentrate too much power in the executive branch, apply to activities that have nothing to do with terrorism, and do little to address the government's mistakes that allowed the September 11 plot to succeed.

Anti-terrorism laws are too broad.
The fundamental problem with laws such as the Patriot Act is the word "terrorism" itself. International lawyer Richard Whitbeck observes:

It is no accident that there is no agreed definition of "terrorism," since the word is so subjective as to be devoid of any inherent meaning. At the same time, the word is extremely dangerous, because people tend to believe that it does have meaning and to use and abuse the word by applying it to whatever they hate as a way of avoiding rational thought and discussion.[2]

Some fear that Section 802 of the act, which defines "domestic terrorism," is so broad that it could lead to a repetition of the intelligence abuses of the 1960s, when government agents spied on antiwar activists and civil rights leaders. The Center for Constitutional Rights warned that, "Rosa Parks, Martin Luther King, Jr., Fred Shuttlesworth, and the activists who stood beside them could have been charged with the crime of domestic terrorism for their acts of nonviolent civil disobedience. Their every move, their political activities, their personal relationships, their financial transactions, and their private records could have been monitored and recorded."[3]

Even though the government calls the Patriot Act an anti-terrorism measure, many of its provisions expand law enforcement powers to fight ordinary crime. In fact, some believe that the Bush administration used the September 11 attacks to pressure Congress into giving prosecutors legal powers that had long been on their "wish list." For example, Section 217 authorizes the monitoring of computers to catch hackers, and Section 503 requires everyone convicted of a violent crime—terrorism-related or not—to provide a sample for the government's national DNA database. The government, by its own admission, has used its new Patriot Act powers "to investigate suspected drug traffickers, white-collar criminals, blackmailers, child pornographers, money launderers, spies, and even corrupt foreign leaders."[4] The Justice Department makes no apologies. A department spokesman said, "I think any reasonable person would agree that we have an obligation to do everything we can to protect the lives and liberties of Americans from attack, whether it's from terrorists or garden-variety criminals."[5]

It is too easy to abuse anti-terrorism laws.

One of the most dangerous features of post–September 11 anti-terrorism laws is that they give the government wide-ranging

Presidential versus Congressional Power: *Youngstown Sheet & Tube Company v. Sawyer*

After the September 11 attacks, President Bush called himself a "war president" and claimed broad powers in the realm of national security. A number of the president's actions have been challenged in court. In resolving these disputes, some judges have turned to Justice Robert Jackson's famous concurring opinion in *Youngstown Sheet & Tube Company v. Sawyer*, 343 U.S. 579, 634 (1952) (Jackson, J., concurring).

The issue in *Youngstown Sheet & Tube* was the president's inherent power as commander in chief. The case arose when steelworkers threatened to call a nationwide strike during the Korean War. To avert the strike, President Harry Truman issued an executive order directing Secretary of Commerce Charles Sawyer to seize and operate most of the mills.

President Truman claimed authority to seize the mills under Article II, Section 2 of the Constitution, which provided that "The President shall be commander in chief of the Army and Navy of the United States." He believed that a steelworkers' strike would jeopardize the nation's defense. The steel companies sued Sawyer in federal court to stop the seizures. The case went to the Supreme Court, which, by a 6 to 3 vote, held that the president did not have the power to seize the mills.

Justice Jackson agreed with the majority but wrote a concurring opinion to explain why. "Presidential powers are not fixed but fluctuate, depending upon their disjunction or conjunction with those of Congress," Jackson explained. He then described the three "zones of presidential power":

1. When the President acts pursuant to an express or implied authorization of Congress, his authority is at its maximum, for it includes all that he possesses in his own right plus all that Congress can delegate. In these circumstances, and in these only, may he be said (for what it may be worth) to personify the federal sovereignty. If his act is held unconstitutional under these circumstances, it usually means that the Federal Government as an undivided whole lacks power. A seizure executed by the President

authority to spy on Americans, even when the focus of the investigation has little or nothing to do with terrorism. Section 213 of the Patriot Act authorizes "sneak-and-peek" searches in

pursuant to an Act of Congress would be supported by the strongest of presumptions and the widest latitude of judicial interpretation, and the burden of persuasion would rest heavily upon any who might attack it.

2. When the President acts in absence of either a congressional grant or denial of authority, he can only rely upon his own independent powers, but there is a zone of twilight in which he and Congress may have concurrent authority, or in which its distribution is uncertain. Therefore, congressional inertia, indifference, or quiescence may sometimes, at least as a practical matter, enable, if not invite, measures on independent presidential responsibility. In this area, any actual test of power is likely to depend on the imperatives of events and contemporary imponderables rather than on abstract theories of law.

3. When the President takes measures incompatible with the expressed or implied will of Congress, his power is at its lowest ebb, for then he can rely only upon his own constitutional powers minus any constitutional powers of Congress over the matter. Courts can sustain exclusive presidential control in such a case only by disabling the Congress from acting upon the subject. Presidential claim to a power at once so conclusive and preclusive must be scrutinized with caution, for what is at stake is the equilibrium established by our constitutional system.

Jess Bravin, a reporter at the *Wall Street Journal*, observed that President Bush's decision to rely on his inherent powers in fighting terrorism came back to haunt him in the form of lawsuits. Bravin wrote:

In the weeks after 9/11, Congress might have armed the president with any power he deemed necessary. But the administration's legal team worried that seeking congressional authorization would implicitly cede lawmakers a power they believed the president already embodied, and could invite future Congresses to regulate matters the White House claimed were exclusively their province.*

*Jess Bravin, "Terror War Legal Edifice Weakens," *Wall Street Journal*, June 13, 2007.

cases involving any federal crime. This means that the government can search first and notify the person searched afterward. Section 216 expands the government's ability to monitor Internet usage, including e-mail addresses used and Web sites visited, in "ongoing criminal investigations," whether terrorism-related or not. The act has also increased the likelihood that innocent people will be spied on. Section 206 allows the FBI to monitor a computer in a public facility, such as a library, if it believes that doing so would lead to information relevant to a criminal investigation. The Internet activity of all users, not just suspects, now can be monitored.

The Patriot Act also gives the government broader access to Americans' personal data. Section 505 authorizes the FBI to issue "national security letters" (NSLs), which are orders directing a holder of business records to turn them over as part of an investigation of suspected terrorist activity. NSLs do not require prior approval by a court, and they can be issued by relatively low-ranking FBI officials. The Justice Department's inspector general, an official responsible for investigating abuse within the department, recently told a congressional committee, "Our review found widespread and serious misuse of the FBI's national security letter authorities. In many instances, the FBI's misuse of national security letters violated NSL statutes, Attorney General Guidelines, or the FBI's own internal policies."[6]

Innocent people have no way of knowing that investigators have been looking at their personal information. Section 206 of the Patriot Act forbids a library or Internet cafe to warn computer users that they are being monitored, and Section 215 imposes a similar "gag order" on keepers of business records. The American Civil Liberties Union, which challenged the constitutionality of Section 215 in court, feared that it could discourage the exercise of free speech. The ACLU said: "There's a real possibility that setting the FBI loose on the American public will have a profound chilling effect on public discourse. If people think that their conversations and their e-mails or their reading habits are being monitored, people will inevitably feel less comfortable saying what they think, especially if what they think is not what the government wants them to think."[7]

Civil liberties groups are concerned about post–September 11 laws that generally make it easier for the government to carry out "foreign intelligence" surveillance, which is governed by fewer legal restrictions than searches for evidence of ordinary crime. The new laws also broaden the government's power to use foreign intelligence surveillance to find evidence of ordinary crime as well as spies and terrorists. As originally enacted, the Foreign Intelligence Surveillance Act of 1978 (FISA) required the government to show that foreign intelligence was "the purpose" of conducting such surveillance. Section 218 of the Patriot Act lowered that standard. All the government now needs to show is that foreign intelligence is "a significant purpose" of the surveillance. In addition, applications for foreign intelligence surveillance are heard by a special court whose judges hear only from lawyers who argue the government's case. That court has reportedly refused only a handful of the government's more than 20,000 applications.

Anti-terrorism laws diminish court supervision of searches in criminal cases. For example, Section 505 of the Patriot Act—the NSL provision—eliminated the requirement of a warrant. In addition, the Protect America Act of 2007 weakened FISA's restrictions on electronic surveillance. The act makes intelligence agencies less accountable to Congress and the courts and thus increases the chances that citizens' communications will be monitored without their knowledge. Civil liberties groups warn that the executive branch will be the judge of the reasonableness of its own actions.

The government has allegedly abused its power in other ways. After September 11, government agents arrested as many as 1,000 Arabs and Muslims. Most were charged with immigration law violations, often minor ones. Only 7 people caught in the sweep were turned over to U.S. marshals to face possible criminal charges. Some of the detainees were held for months, denied access to a lawyer, or mistreated while in custody. Human rights groups sued the government for details about the roundup, but in *Center for National Security Studies v. Department of Justice*, 331 F.3d 918 (D.C. Cir. 2003), a federal appeals court ruled for the government. The court agreed with the government that releasing the information—even the names of those detained—would endanger national security. Judge David Tatel, who dissented, suggested that the government might have covered up its violations of the law. He wrote: "History . . . is full of examples of situations in which just these sorts of allegations led to the discovery of serious government wrongdoing—from Teapot Dome in the 1920s to the FBI's COINTELPRO counterintelligence program in the 1960s to Watergate in the 1970s."[8]

The Justice Department and other agencies have argued repeatedly that national security requires them to operate in secret. Professor Ronald Dworkin replies, "This is an argument made by every police state, and it may be the most self-serving and indefensible claim the Bush administration has made so far."[9]

Laws alone will not prevent terrorist attacks.

The Patriot Act has made it easier for law enforcement agencies to collect information they think is relevant to terrorist activity, and to share it with one another. Some critics insist that the government is missing the point. They question whether more information, by itself, will prevent another attack, and go on to argue that gathering more information might make it even more difficult to find terrorists. For example, the government's "Visa Condor" program, which began shortly after the September 11 attacks, screened more than 100,000 Arab and Muslim men who applied for American visas. The program found no terrorists and created a backlash that hurt this country's tourism industry.

Many observers insist that the biggest problem is not a lack of information, but rather a lack of trained personnel—especially personnel capable of reading and speaking Arabic—who can analyze the information that agencies already have.

One major reason why the September 11 attackers succeeded was that the government failed to act on the information that it already had. A study by the Merkel Family Foundation found that two of the hijackers' names were on a government list of suspected terrorists, and that further data checks—for example, looking for the people who lived at the same address, used the same phone number, or had the same frequent flyer number as the two suspects—might have identified other members of the plot. Some have also suggested that before asking for new laws, the authorities should do a better job of enforcing those already on the books. Critics complain that immigration authorities were especially lax; for example, they allowed foreign visitors to overstay their visas and did not pressure universities to obey laws requiring them to turn over information about foreign students.

The risk of terrorism has been exaggerated.

Long before the September 11 attacks, there was widespread fear of terrorism. In 1986, Americans rated it as their primary concern, even though terrorism was far down on the list of causes of death to Americans. As George McGovern and William Polk point out, "Even if you include 9/11 casualties, the number of Americans being killed by international terrorists since the late 1960s (which is when the State Department began counting them) is about the same as that of killed by lightning—or by accident-causing deer, or by severe allergic reactions to peanuts."[10] Even in 2001, drunk drivers claimed many more lives than terrorists. According to the Department of Transportation, 17,448 people died that year in alcohol-related crashes.[11]

John Mueller, a professor of history at Ohio State University, argues that the United States overreacted to the September 11

Personal Justice Denied: The Japanese Internment Cases

In the months after Pearl Harbor, the Japanese military swept across the western Pacific, leading to fears that the West Coast of the United States might be attacked. The U.S. military was also concerned that some of the more than 100,000 ethnic Japanese living on the West Coast would side with the enemy.

In February 1942, President Roosevelt issued an executive order authorizing military commanders to take steps they considered necessary to prevent espionage and sabotage. Shortly afterward, Congress made disobedience of military restrictions a misdemeanor, thus allowing civilian courts to sentence violators. Acting under the president's order, military authorities imposed a nighttime curfew on ethnic Japanese living in military zones and later ordered them to report to relocation centers. Those were the first steps in the process of interning the Japanese in camps hundreds of miles away from the West Coast. Court challenges to those restrictions led to two of the most controversial decisions in Supreme Court history.

The first case involved Kiyoshi Hirabayashi, a college student living in Seattle. Hirabayashi appealed his conviction for violating the curfew and failing to report to a relocation center. He argued that the military orders discriminated against him on account of his ethnicity. The case went up to the Supreme Court, which, in *Hirabayashi v. United States*, 320 U.S. 81 (1943), unanimously upheld his conviction.

The court's opinion, written by Chief Justice Harlan Stone, rested on the principle that courts deferred to the other branches of government in matters related to war. The chief justice found that the military had reason to believe ethnic Japanese would sabotage the war effort and that a curfew was an appropriate means of preventing it. Although racial discrimination was usually prohibited, it was permissible if "residents having different ethnic affiliations with an invading enemy may be a greater source of danger than those of a different ancestry."

The *Hirabayashi* court put off ruling on the constitutionality of the forced relocation of ethnic Japanese. Because Hirabayashi had been sentenced to concurrent jail terms for violating two different orders, the court only needed to find one of them—the curfew order—constitutional, postponing the issue of whether the government could force the Japanese into camps.

The court was forced to decide that issue in *Korematsu v. United States*, 323 U.S. 214 (1944). Toyosaburo Korematsu appealed his conviction for refusing to leave

San Leandro, California, a military area from which ethnic Japanese were excluded. Korematsu's appeal went to the Supreme Court, which, by a 6 to 3 vote, upheld his conviction.

Justice Hugo Black's majority opinion focused on Korematsu's exclusion. He wrote: "Regardless of the true nature of the assembly and relocation centers—and we deem it unjustifiable to call them concentration camps with all the ugly connotations that term implies—we are dealing specifically with nothing but an exclusion order." He concluded that even though restrictions aimed at a single racial group deserved "the most rigid scrutiny," the wartime exclusion of ethnic Japanese from a threatened area had "a definite and close relationship to the prevention of espionage and sabotage." Although the United States was by that time winning the war, Justice Black refused to second-guess the military's determination in 1942 that there were disloyal Japanese whose exclusion was necessary.

The three dissenting justices condemned the unequal treatment of ethnic Japanese. Justice Owen Roberts also accused the majority of avoiding the real issue: forcing people into camps solely because of their ancestry and without evidence that they were disloyal. Justice Frank Murphy questioned the military's contention that the relocation was necessary to prevent sabotage. Justice Robert Jackson argued that the court had made a mistake by deciding the constitutionality of the president's military orders in the first place. He believed that it would have been wiser to let the voters, not the courts, serve as the ultimate check on the president's use of his war powers.

The same day it decided *Korematsu*, the court also decided *Ex Parte Endo*, 323 U.S. 283 (1944), which concluded that the interment of at least some Japanese Americans was unconstitutional. Mitsuye Endo, a Japanese American who had been transported to a camp in Utah, filed a habeas corpus petition. The court unanimously sided with Endo, finding that the government had conceded her loyalty yet delayed her release because local officials feared an uncontrolled migration of ethnic Japanese into their communities. Speaking for a unanimous court, Justice William Douglas wrote, "A citizen who is concededly loyal presents no problem of espionage or sabotage. Loyalty is a matter of the heart and mind not of race, creed, or color. He who is loyal is by definition not a spy or a saboteur."

Reading *Korematsu* and *Endo* together, the court concluded that a Japanese American had no right to defy the military's relocation order, but, once interned

(continues)

(continued)

in a camp, could file a habeas corpus petition alleging that he or she was a loyal citizen and therefore detained unlawfully. Many believe that this awkward result supports the notion that the court should have avoided ruling on the constitutionality of the president's military orders in the first place. Former Chief Justice William Rehnquist observed, "If, in fact, courts are more prone to uphold wartime claims of civil liberties after the war is over, may it not actually be desirable to avoid decision on such claims during the war?"*

In any event, historians consider the Japanese internment one of the more shameful episodes in American legal history. In 1983, a federal commission issued a report titled *Personal Justice Denied*, which concluded that the internment was not justified by military necessity and that the Supreme Court decisions upholding it had been "overruled in the court of history." The following year, U.S. District Judge Marilyn Patel issued an order vacating Korematsu's conviction. In doing so, she concluded that the claim of military necessity for President Roosevelt's order was based on "unsubstantiated facts, distortions, and representations of at least one military commander, whose views were seriously infected by racism."**

* William H. Rehnquist, *All Laws But One: Civil Liberties in Wartime*. New York: Alfred A. Knopf, 1998: p. 222.

** Commission on Wartime Relocation and Internment of Civilians, *Personal Justice Denied*. Washington, D.C.: Government Printing Office, 1982.

attacks and, by doing so, added to the damage caused by the attacks themselves. "The chief costs of terrorism derive not from the damage inflicted by the terrorists, but what those attacked do to themselves and others in response," Mueller said.[12] He adds that the money spent on counterterrorism measures—including some, such as passenger screening at airports, which arguably do little to prevent an attack—could have been put to better use vaccinating Americans against bird flu, responding to Hurricane Katrina, or fighting violent crime. The 9/11 Commission concluded that it is impossible to reduce the risk of another terrorist attack to zero. Mueller elaborates: "Terrorism is therefore much more like crime than war. Like crime, terrorism has always existed and always will, and the best hope is to reduce its frequency and consequences sufficiently that people come to feel generally, though never completely, safe from it."[13]

Critics accuse political leaders of using the threat of more attacks to frighten the public into giving up its freedom. They believe that the erosion of civil liberties, and the climate of fear that accompanies it, represents an abandonment of what defines Americans as Americans in the first place. Russ Feingold, the only senator to vote against the Patriot Act, explained, "The Founders who wrote our Constitution and Bill of Rights exercised that vigilance even though they had recently fought and won the Revolutionary War. They did not live in comfortable and easy times of hypothetical enemies. They wrote a Constitution of limited powers and an explicit Bill of Rights to protect liberty in times of war, as well as in times of peace."[14]

Anti-terrorism laws encourage discrimination.

In past conflicts, members of minority groups have suffered from abuse of government power. German Americans were targeted during World War I; Japanese Americans during World War II; and in the current fight against terrorists, the scapegoats are Arabs and Muslims, who were viewed with suspicion even before September 11. Senator Feingold warned that this would happen. He said, "Who do we think is most likely to bear the brunt of the abuse? It won't be immigrants from Ireland. It won't be immigrants from El Salvador or Nicaragua. It won't even be immigrants from Haiti or Africa. It will be immigrants from Arab, Muslim, and South Asian countries."[15]

After the September 11 attacks, federal agents interviewed thousands of Arab and Muslim men who felt they had no choice but to cooperate. Many were jailed and deported, often for immigration offenses once considered "technical." The crackdown, which some call a classic case of racial profiling, was not limited to immigrants. Arab-Americans reported a sharp increase in incidents of discrimination and harassment, especially multiple searches and identification checks at airports, a phenomenon they called "flying while brown." Georgetown University law professor David Cole was highly critical of the government's heavy-handed tactics: "What the government has done, again, is to take its tremendously broad power over foreign nationals and use it as a pretext to round up specific groups—in this case Arabs and Muslims. . . . The result, to date, is virtually no new terrorists identified, no further participants in 9/11 identified, and a deeply alienated community."[16] Many contend that the government did more harm than good by making Arabs and Muslims suspicious of the government at a time when their cooperation was most needed.

Former Vice President Al Gore called the government's actions a "cheap and cruel publicity stunt." He said, "More than 99% of the mostly Arab-background men who were rounded up had merely overstayed their visas or committed some other minor offense. . . . But they were used as extras in the Administration's effort to give the impression that they had caught a large number of bad guys."[17]

Summary

The war on terror has resulted in laws that give national security and law enforcement agencies broader powers and, at the same time, diminished the role of courts in guarding against the abuse of power. Laws aimed at terrorism have been used to pursue ordinary criminals, and have given the government more power to target members of minority groups and spy on innocent citizens. At the same time, the government has become more secretive, and the added secrecy has made it more difficult to expose abuses of power. Critics believe that the government's new powers erode civil liberties, but at the same time do little to address the intelligence failures that led to the September 11 attacks. Some also maintain that the government overreacted to the terrorism threat and is ignoring other, even more serious dangers to this country.

The Future of the War on Terror

After the September 11 attacks, President Bush described the problem that the country faces: "In a globalized world, events beyond America's borders have a greater impact inside them. . . . The characteristics we most cherish—our freedom, our cities, our systems of movement, and modern life—are vulnerable to terrorism."[1]

The president described terrorism as "a new condition of life" and warned that people will be vulnerable even after those responsible for the September 11 attacks are brought to justice. Since that day, there has been considerable debate over whether the country is safer now than it was before the attacks; what impact the war in Iraq has had on the fight against terrorism; and, looking to the future, what is the best way to combat terrorism at home and abroad.

Legal and Political Issues

The government's anti-terrorism strategy has led to disagreements among political leaders and legal experts, as well as lawsuits challenging the government's new powers. The principal legal and political issues include these:

The Patriot Act and Other Anti-terrorism Legislation

After Congress passed the Patriot Act in 2001, civil liberties groups objected vigorously and hundreds of communities—as well as several state legislatures—passed resolutions protesting the law. However, opposition diminished with the passage of time. The renewal legislation, passed in 2006, made relatively minor amendments to the original act. Nevertheless, some remain opposed to the law. Russ Feingold, the only senator to vote against the act in 2001, complained that the renewal did little to protect librarians and keepers of business records and did nothing to curb sneak-and-peak searches. The Patriot Act is not the only concern of civil libertarians. The administration's reported monitoring of Americans' telephone and e-mail conversations, possibly in violation of federal statutes, has added to fears that the government is misusing the additional power it attained to combat terrorism.

On the other hand, many Americans, including members of the Bush administration, contend that even the Patriot Act did not give the government all of the tools it needs to combat terrorism. The president has called on Congress to expand the FBI's authority to obtain information without a court order, to deny bail to accused terrorists, and to make additional terrorism-related crimes punishable by death.

Those and other provisions appeared in a Justice Department draft of the Domestic Security Enhancement Act, or "Patriot Act II," which was leaked to a Washington-based advocacy group in 2003. Patriot Act II would further expand the scope of government surveillance and permit the government to act with greater secrecy and less supervision by the courts. Even though Patriot Act II, per se, never came to the floor of either house of Congress, portions of it have become law over the years: For example, the Intelligence Reform Act of 2004 authorized surveillance of suspected "lone wolf" terrorists—people such as the Unabomber—who are not associated with any foreign power. The Real ID Act of 2005 made it easier to deport non-citizens who are suspected of terrorist activity. The legislation that renewed the Patriot Act also expanded post-release supervision of convicted terrorists.

Collection and Use of Personal Information

One issue in the controversy over National Security Agency (NSA) surveillance of suspected terrorist activity involved "data mining," the analysis of large amounts of personal information stored in public and government computers. Generally speaking, the purpose of data mining is to discover hidden patterns, or "profiles," inside large collections of data. Businesses mine data to identify customers who respond to their advertising or who buy certain products. The government has used data mining to detect fraud and, more recently, to find terrorists.

Defenders of data mining argue that it can focus scarce resources on finding terrorists. If precautions are taken to protect the identities of innocent subjects, data mining can also reduce the risk of discrimination against members of minority groups. Opponents warn, however, that data mining is not foolproof. The risks include poor data quality; "mission creep," or mining data to find non-terrorist offenders such as tax evaders; human errors in interpreting data; and "false positives," in which a non-terrorist is identified as one.

Another controversial program that was developed after the September 11 attacks is CAPPS II. This program relies on a computer analysis of government and commercial databases to assign a "security rating" to airline passengers. Critics argued that CAPPS II was too expensive, endangered privacy, and would not catch terrorists. In 2007, Congress ordered the Department of Homeland Security not to spend money on programs that create security ratings on people who are not already on a terrorist watch list.

National Identity Cards

After the attacks, it was discovered that police had stopped four of the September 11 hijackers while they were illegally in this country. But none of the men were investigated further. These incidents led the 9/11 Commission to call for more secure borders and tougher enforcement of the immigration laws. The commission did not recommend national identity cards, but David Frum and Richard Perle argue that the cards are needed. They wrote:

> [T]here is only one system that will do the job: a national identity card that registers the bearer's name and biometric data, like fingerprints or retinal scans or DNA, and that indicates whether the bearer is a citizen, a permanent resident, or a temporary resident—and, if temporary, would indicate whether the bearer is permitted to work and the date by which he or she is supposed to leave. [2]

Frum and Perle draw a distinction between privacy and invisibility, and argue that terrorists want to be invisible. On the other hand, opponents of identity cards contend that asking citizens for "your papers, please," is the hallmark of a police state, not a free country such as the United States. They add that an identity card requirement will lead to racial profiling and other harassment, and in any event would not stop sophisticated terrorists from creating false identities.

Profiling

After September 11, some observers argued in favor of profiling, the practice of concentrating law enforcement efforts on those people who meet a set of criteria associated with certain crimes. Those criteria often involve one's physical appearance. Profiling has come under attack when studies revealed that African Americans are more likely to be stopped by the police, especially while driving. However, advocates believe that profiling is not only smart police work, but also essential to fighting terrorist acts such as airplane hijackings. Conservative talk show host Michael Smerconish is critical of airlines for not profiling their passengers. On a family trip to Florida, Smerconish's eight-year-old son was selected for "secondary screening" on both legs of the flight. In his book *Flying Blind*, Smerconish argued:

> We're fighting a war against young Arab male extremists, and yet our government continues to enforce politically correct "random screening" of airline passengers instead of targeting those who look like terrorists. Why? Because they don't want to hurt anyone's feelings. Essentially, they are putting more emphasis on protecting diversity than protecting our safety.[3]

Opponents believe that profiling does not work because terrorists will outsmart profilers. According to former Congressman Bob Barr, "As the CIA itself noted in an unclassified study reportedly conducted in 2001, terrorists typically take great pains to avoid being profiled: they don't want to get caught, and in fact it is essentially impossible to profile terrorists."[4] Those who oppose profiling cite the examples of Jose Padilla, who was recently convicted of aiding terrorists, and Richard Reid, the would-be "shoe bomber." Neither man fit the physical profile of a Middle Easterner.

A Clash of Civilizations?

In 1993, political scientist Samuel Huntington wrote a controversial article, "The Clash of Civilizations," in *Foreign Affairs* magazine. Huntington observed, "The great divisions among humankind and the dominating source of conflict will be cultural. . . . The clash of civilizations will dominate global politics. The fault lines between civilizations will be the battle lines of the future."[5] Huntington asserted that the clash between the Western and Islamic worlds has been going on for more than a millennium and has intensified since the end of the Cold War. Recent armed conflicts associated with the clash include those in Bosnia and Chechnya.

Conflict has also occurred outside the cultural "fault lines." In 2004, a fundamentalist Muslim fatally shot Dutch filmmaker Theo Van Gogh in downtown Amsterdam. Van Gogh was a vocal critic of the Islamic faith. The Dutch people reacted to the assassination by endorsing tougher anti-crime measures and a harder line toward immigration. Elsewhere in Europe, there have been demonstrations protesting a Danish newspaper's publication of cartoons depicting the prophet Muhammad, cartoons that Muslims consider sacrilegious. There has also been bitter debate over whether girls may wear Islamic headscarves to public schools, and the extent to which Muslim clerics should be allowed to preach anti-Western messages to their congregations.

Huntington's "clash of civilizations" theory is controversial. Some fear that his views can be used to justify the kind of discrimination against Arabs and Muslims that occurred after September 11 and—worse still—that it adds to the perception that Westerners and Muslims can never live in peace. (Huntington believes that coexistence is possible, but that it will be difficult.) Others insist that a cultural clash is unavoidable. They point to the spread of "political Islam," a radical ideology that views the United States as an "evil empire" and opposes Western ideas such as democracy and capitalism. Political Islam is attracting young Muslims, even those who are not strongly religious, because they see the fight against terrorism as an attack on them. Some believe that much of the Muslim world, not just al Qaeda, is at war with the United States. In 2003, an editorial in a New York City newspaper stated:

America is hated and feared by the clerical and political classes—the only ones that matter—from North Africa to Southeast Asia.

The Trials of Jose Padilla

President Bush told the nation in September 2001 that the fight against terrorism was "a new kind of war." The case of Jose Padilla exposed some of the legal issues that can arise in such a war.

Padilla was an American citizen, born in New York. After he served a prison term on a weapons charge, he adopted the Muslim faith, changing his name to Abdullah al-Muhajir. Padilla also traveled overseas, including to Afghanistan where he allegedly attended al Qaeda training camps and met the leaders of that organization.

In May 2002, FBI agents arrested Padilla at Chicago's O'Hare Airport after he got off a flight from Pakistan. While Padilla was in custody, President Bush issued an order designating him an enemy combatant and had him moved to a military prison in South Carolina. The government argued that Padilla was involved with al Qaeda and had been sent back to America to commit terrorist acts, including detonating a "dirty bomb," a conventional weapon packed with radioactive waste designed to disperse into the air when the bomb went off. The government also argued that Padilla possessed important intelligence about al Qaeda.

A federal appeals court ruled that the president had no authority to detain an American citizen who had been seized on American soil outside a combat zone. The government appealed that decision to the U.S. Supreme Court, which, in *Padilla v. Rumsfeld*, 524 U.S. 426 (2004), refused to rule on the merits of the case. It concluded that Padilla had filed his habeas corpus petition in the wrong jurisdiction: New York, where he was originally taken into custody, rather than South Carolina, where he was being held at the time.

Padilla's lawyers started over in South Carolina, where the district court ruled in his favor. However, in *Padilla v. Hanft*, 423 F.3d 386 (4th Cir. 2005), the U.S. Circuit Court of Appeals for the Fourth Circuit ruled unanimously in favor of the government. Judge Michael Luttig wrote the panel's opinion. He concluded that the 2001 Authorization for the Use of Military Force (AUMF) resolution gave the president the power to take al Qaeda fighters into custody and detain them until the end of the conflict. Judge Luttig also concluded that Padilla's American citizenship did not exempt him from military justice. Finally, Luttig found it irrelevant that

This hatred is so widespread and powerful that it unites ancient rivals. Sunnis and Shiites, Persians and Arabs, Baathists and royalists, tribal leaders and urban intellectuals,

---

Padilla had been captured in the United States rather than Afghanistan because he was just as likely to rejoin the enemy as a fighter who had been captured on the battlefield itself.

The legal proceedings took an unexpected turn in November 2005 after a federal grand jury indicted Padilla and four other men. The indictment charged Padilla with acts that were considerably different from, and less serious than, the alleged actions that led to his military detention. It accused the men of raising money and recruiting volunteers during the 1990s to fight in Chechnya, Somalia, and the former Yugoslavia. Padilla appeared to have played a minor role in the conspiracy.

After Padilla was indicted, the government asked the Fourth Circuit to end the habeas corpus case and allow it to transfer Padilla to civilian authorities. In *Padilla v. Hanft*, No. 05–6396 (U.S. Ct. App., 4th Cir., Dec. 21, 2005), the appeals court refused. Judge Luttig expressed his displeasure with the government, suggesting that it wanted to avoid a Supreme Court ruling on whether Padilla could be kept in military custody. Shortly afterward, however, the Supreme Court gave the government permission to move Padilla to civilian custody.

Before his conspiracy trial began, Padilla argued that he was not mentally competent to stand trial as a result of being tortured in prison. He told the court that his interrogators "confin[ed] him in a 9-by-7-foot cell with no natural light, no clock, and no calendar for nearly four years. Whenever Padilla left the cell, he was shackled and suited in heavy goggles and headphones. He was forbidden contact with anyone but his interrogators, who punctured the extreme sensory deprivation with sensory overload, blasting him with harsh lights and pounding sounds."* Author Naomi Klein argued that Padilla's interrogation was not an isolated case. She said that the United States might have tortured thousands of other prisoners whose stories will never be told because they were held outside the jurisdiction of American courts.

In August 2007, a federal court jury in Florida found Padilla guilty of conspiracy to murder, kidnap, and maim people overseas, and two counts of providing material support to terrorists. He was later sentenced to 17 years in prison.

* Naomi Klein, "A Trial for Thousands Denied Trial," *The Nation*, March 12, 2007.

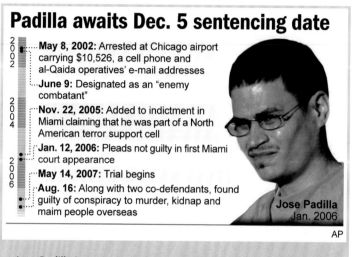

Padilla awaits Dec. 5 sentencing date

2002

- **May 8, 2002:** Arrested at Chicago airport carrying $10,526, a cell phone and al-Qaida operatives' e-mail addresses
- **June 9:** Designated as an "enemy combatant"

2004

- **Nov. 22, 2005:** Added to indictment in Miami claiming that he was part of a North American terror support cell
- **Jan. 12, 2006:** Pleads not guilty in first Miami court appearance

2006

- **May 14, 2007:** Trial begins
- **Aug. 16:** Along with two co-defendants, found guilty of conspiracy to murder, kidnap and maim people overseas

Jose Padilla
Jan. 2006

AP

Jose Padilla is an American citizen who converted to Islam. He also allegedly traveled to Afghanistan and trained in al Qaeda's camps. When Padilla returned to the United States, he was arrested and designated an enemy combatant, which started a series of legal actions, summarized above.

theologians and supposedly secular military officers—all gather under the banner of jihad.[6]

Other Terrorist Threats

Americans associate terrorism with the Middle East or, more specifically, with al Qaeda. However, experts believe that radical Muslims will not be the only terrorists of the future. There are a variety of predictions about the changing face of terrorism. In 1999, the United States Commission on National Security warned that civil wars will breed new terrorist movements and weaken some governments to the point that they can no longer control terrorist organizations. Parts of Southeast Asia, South America, and especially Africa could be the home of future terrorists. Meanwhile, experts warn of a rising danger from home-grown terrorists such as Timothy McVeigh or the Unabomber.

In July 2007, a National Intelligence Estimate (NIE) prepared by the U.S. intelligence community noted that "single issue" groups might resort to violence. Author, historian, and terrorism expert Walter Laqueur thinks that future terrorists are more likely to be "lone wolves" with weapons of mass destruction, similar to the "mad scientists" in old science fiction movies.

Experts offer a variety of ideas about future terrorists' weapons of choice, but generally agree that the primary concern is WMDs. The 2007 NIE stated: "We assess that al Qaeda will continue to try to acquire and employ chemical, biological, radiological, or nuclear material in attacks and would not hesitate to use them if it develops what it deems is sufficient capability."[7] Laqueur warned of another, potentially more destructive threat: "cyber-terrorism." In March 2007, researchers at the U.S. Department of Energy launched an experimental attack that exposed the vulnerability of the nation's electrical infrastructure. Experts believe that terrorists could launch simultaneous cyber attacks on key facilities and leave a large part of this country without power for months. Scott Borg, an economist who provides security-related data to the federal government, warned that the economic consequences of such an attack would be catastrophic: "It's equivalent to 40 to 50 large hurricanes striking all at once . . . It's greater economic damage than any modern economy ever suffered . . . It's greater than the Great Depression. It's greater than the damage we did with strategic bombing on Germany in World War II."[8]

The September 11 attacks were designed to inflict mass casualties and attract international attention. Many experts believe that al Qaeda intends to stage another attack of equal or greater magnitude, though they disagree as to the organization's ability to do so in the near future. At the same time, experts believe that some terrorists have changed their tactics and will stage smaller-scale attacks that are harder to detect and prevent.

The Madrid railroad station bombings in 2004 appear to have been the work of "self-starters," local extremists who were not directed by high al Qaeda officials but who instead planned the attack locally. Experts believe that the Internet makes it easier for terrorist cells to recruit members, exchange information about targets, and learn how to make bombs and other weapons. The 2007 NIE stated:

> We assess that globalization trends and recent technological advances will continue to enable even small numbers of alienated people to find and connect with one another, justify and intensify their anger, and mobilize resources to attack—all without requiring a centralized terrorist organization, training camp, or leader.[9]

Battling for Hearts and Minds

Experts warn that military force alone will not eliminate the terrorist threat. The British, who have faced terrorists around the world, learned the hard way that fighting terrorism is a struggle for "hearts and minds" and that the misuse of force, such as firing on Irish Republican Army (IRA) demonstrators on "Bloody Sunday" in 1972, provides terrorists with a propaganda victory.

Some question whether the West is doing enough to win hearts and minds in the Middle East and warn that a generation is being created of extremists who see terrorism as the only way to fight back. A memo by former Defense Secretary Donald Rumsfeld suggested that the fight against terrorism could be lost. He wrote: "Are we capturing, killing, or deterring and dissuading more terrorists every day than the *madrassas* [Islamic religious schools] and the radical clerics are recruiting, training, and deploying against us? The cost-benefit ratio is against us! Our cost is billions against the terrorists' costs of millions."[10] Critics of U.S. counterterrorism policy maintain that the government is doing too little to address the root causes of terrorism. They urge the United States to stop supporting corrupt dictatorships, help countries build economies based on brainpower rather than on oil, and pursue a more evenhanded peace policy in the Middle East.

The Future of the War on Terror

After the September 11 attacks, President Bush told Congress, "Our war on terror begins with al Qaeda, but it does not end there. It will not end until every terrorist group of global reach has been found, stopped, and defeated."[11] Most Americans expect a long conflict. According to a CBS News poll taken two years after the attacks, 24 percent of Americans said they believed the war on terror would last longer than 10 years, and another 34 percent believed it would last "a long time" or "forever."

Because the war on terror is a lower-intensity conflict than recent conventional wars, some are uncomfortable with calling it a "war." James Fallows believes that doing so is counter-productive:

> It cheapens the concept of war, making the word a synonym for effort or goal. It predisposes us toward overreactions, of the kind that have already proved so harmful. . . .
>
> A state of war encourages a state of fear. . . .
>
> A state of war also predisposes the United States to think about using its assets in a strictly warlike way—and to give short shrift to the vast range of their other possibilities. . . .
>
> Perhaps worst of all, an open-ended war is an open-ended invitation to defeat.[12]

Victor Davis Hanson takes the opposite view. Shortly after the attacks, he argued:

> [B]y any fair historical measure when three thousand innocents have been butchered in a time of peace by enemies of our very civilization—in addition to $100 billion of material losses, more still in economic dislocation, and our symbols of American internationalism, military power, and finance blown apart—then, by God, we are in a war.[13]

Experts disagree as to whether the war on terror is being won. Five years after the September 11 attacks, James Fallows talked to 60 terrorism experts. Many told him that anti-terrorism measures by the United States and the international community—as well as mistakes on the part of al Qaeda, such as launching attacks that killed innocent Muslims—have weakened al Qaeda's ability to stage another major attack. However, Daniel Benjamin and Steven Simon warn that al Qaeda is regaining strength:

> It is simply no longer possible to say that the United States is winning the war on terror. The number of terrorists is growing, as is the pool of people who may be moved to violence, and the means and know-how for carrying out attacks, including catastrophic ones, are becoming more readily available.[14]

America's immediate problem remains al Qaeda and terrorist groups affiliated with and trained by it. In 2002, Benjamin and Simon laid out a strategy to defeat it: "For the next few years, the objective . . . will be to contain the threat, much as the United States contained Soviet power throughout the Cold War. The adversary must be prevented from doing his worst, while the United States and its allies wear down his capabilities and undermine the support he derives from coreligionists."[15] They also advised the United States to "convince Muslim populations that they can prosper without either destroying the West or abandoning their traditions to the onslaught of Western culture."[16]

However the fight against terrorism is labeled, an important question remains: How and when will it end? Some compare it to the Vietnam War, which was as much a struggle for hearts and minds as for supremacy on the battlefield. Others liken it to the Thirty Years' War (1618–1648), a bloody conflict between Catholic and Protestant rulers that did not end until millions of Europeans were dead and the warring sides were too exhausted to fight. Still others think the fight against terror is a modern-day version of the Cold War, a "long twilight struggle" that lasted for more than a generation and finally ended with the collapse of communism. Experts have differing opinions on how the war on terror should be fought, but they do agree on one thing: It will be a difficult and drawn-out conflict.

Summary

The war on terror has led to debate about whether additional government powers are needed at home and about the best way to deal with terrorists overseas. Domestic policy issues include the extent of surveillance aimed at finding terrorists and who in the government ought to oversee it; whether Americans should carry national identification cards; and whether it is acceptable to focus law enforcement efforts on specific nationalities and ethnic groups. Foreign policy issues include whether the fight against terror can be won by force alone, whether the West is winning the hearts and minds of Arabs and Muslims, and whether the United States has done enough to address the root causes of terrorism. Meanwhile, Americans will continue to debate such questions as what is the best way to defeat al Qaeda and how the risk of another attack can be minimized.

Beginning Legal Research

The goals of each book in the Point-Counterpoint series are not only to give the reader a basic introduction to a controversial issue affecting society, but also to encourage the reader to explore the issue more fully. This Appendix is meant to serve as a guide to the reader in researching the current state of the law as well as exploring some of the public policy arguments as to why existing laws should be changed or new laws are needed.

Although some sources of law can be found primarily in law libraries, legal research has become much faster and more accessible with the advent of the Internet. This Appendix discusses some of the best starting points for free access to laws and court decisions, but surfing the Web will uncover endless additional sources of information. Before you can research the law, however, you must have a basic understanding of the American legal system.

The most important source of law in the United States is the Constitution. Originally enacted in 1787, the Constitution outlines the structure of our federal government, as well as setting limits on the types of laws that the federal government and state governments can enact. Through the centuries, a number of amendments have added to or changed the Constitution, most notably the first 10 amendments, which collectively are known as the "Bill of Rights" and which guarantee important civil liberties.

Reading the plain text of the Constitution provides little information. For example, the Constitution prohibits "unreasonable searches and seizures" by the police. To understand concepts in the Constitution, it is necessary to look to the decisions of the U.S. Supreme Court, which has the ultimate authority in interpreting the meaning of the Constitution. For example, the U.S. Supreme Court's 2001 decision in Kyllo v. United States held that scanning the outside of a person's house using a heat sensor to determine whether the person is growing marijuana is an unreasonable search—if it is done without first getting a search warrant from a judge. Each state also has its own constitution and a supreme court that is the ultimate authority on its meaning.

Also important are the written laws, or "statutes," passed by the U.S. Congress and the individual state legislatures. As with constitutional provisions, the U.S. Supreme Court and the state supreme courts are the ultimate authorities in interpreting the meaning of federal and state laws, respectively. However, the U.S. Supreme Court might find that a state law violates the U.S. Constitution, and a state supreme court might find that a state law violates either the state or U.S. Constitution.

Not every controversy reaches either the U.S. Supreme Court or the state supreme courts, however. Therefore, the decisions of other courts are also important. Trial courts hear evidence from both sides and make a decision, while appeals courts review the decisions made by trial courts. Sometimes rulings from appeals courts are appealed further to the U.S. Supreme Court or the state supreme courts.

Lawyers and courts refer to statutes and court decisions through a formal system of citations. Use of these citations reveals which court made the decision or which legislature passed the statute, and allows one to quickly locate the statute or court case online or in a law library. For example, the Supreme Court case Brown v. Board of Education has the legal citation 347 U.S. 483 (1954). At a law library, this 1954 decision can be found on page 483 of volume 347 of the U.S. Reports, which are the official collection of the Supreme Court's decisions. On the following page, you will find sample of all the major kinds of legal citation.

Finding sources of legal information on the Internet is relatively simple thanks to "portal" sites such as findlaw.com and lexisone.com, which allow the user to access a variety of constitutions, statutes, court opinions, law review articles, news articles, and other useful sources of information. For example, findlaw.com offers access to all Supreme Court decisions since 1893. Other useful sources of information include gpo.gov, which contains a complete copy of the U.S. Code, and thomas.loc.gov, which offers access to bills pending before Congress, as well as recently passed laws. Of course, the Internet changes every second of every day, so it is best to do some independent searching.

Of course, many people still do their research at law libraries, some of which are open to the public. For example, some state governments and universities offer the public access to their law collections. Law librarians can be of great assistance, as even experienced attorneys need help with legal research from time to time.

Common Citation Forms

Source of Law	Sample Citation	Notes
U.S. Supreme Court	*Employment Division v. Smith*, 485 U.S. 660 (1988)	The U.S. Reports is the official record of Supreme Court decisions. There is also an unofficial Supreme Court ("S. Ct.") reporter.
U.S. Court of Appeals	*United States v. Lambert*, 695 F.2d 536 (11th Cir.1983)	Appellate cases appear in the Federal Reporter, designated by "F." The 11th Circuit has jurisdiction in Alabama, Florida, and Georgia.
U.S. District Court	*Carillon Importers, Ltd. v. Frank Pesce Group, Inc.*, 913 F.Supp. 1559 (S.D.Fla.1996)	Federal trial-level decisions are reported in the Federal Supplement ("F. Supp."). Some states have multiple federal districts; this case originated in the Southern District of Florida.
U.S. Code	Thomas Jefferson Commemoration Commission Act, 36 U.S.C., §149 (2002)	Sometimes the popular names of legislation—names with which the public may be familiar—are included with the U.S. Code citation.
State Supreme Court	*Sterling v. Cupp*, 290 Ore. 611, 614, 625 P.2d 123, 126 (1981)	The Oregon Supreme Court decision is reported in both the state's reporter and the Pacific regional reporter.
State Statute	Pennsylvania Abortion Control Act of 1982, 18 Pa. Cons. Stat. 3203-3220 (1990)	States use many different citation formats for their statutes.

Cases

Al-Marri v. Wright, 487 F.3d 160 (4th Cir. 2007)

Ruled that an individual who was merely associated with al Qaeda but did not fight alongside it could not be detained as an unlawful combatant. The full Fourth Circuit has agreed to hear the government's appeal in this case.

Boumediene v. Bush, 476 F.3d 981 (D.C. Cir. 2007)

Concluded that the Military Commissions Act barred the federal courts from hearing Guantanamo detainees' habeas corpus petitions. The Supreme Court will hear an appeal of this decision.

Ex Parte Milligan, 71 U.S. 2 (1866)

Held that an individual who had not taken up arms against the country, at a time when habeas corpus remained in force and the civilian courts were open, could not be tried by a military commission.

Ex Parte Quirin, 317 U.S. 1 (1942)

Upheld the use of a military commission to try agents of the German Reich who had entered the United States in order to commit sabotage during World War II.

Hamdan v. Rumsfeld, 548 U.S.—, 165 L.Ed.2d 723 (2006)

Held that the military commissions created by President Bush violated the Geneva Conventions and the federal Uniform Code of Military Justice. Congress addressed the court's objections by enacting the Military Commissions Act of 2006.

Hamdi v. Rumsfeld, 542 U.S. 507 (2004)

Upheld the president's authority to detain unlawful combatants, but ruled that an American citizen has the right to a hearing on his unlawful combatant status.

In re Sealed Case, 310 F.3d 717 (For. Int. Surv. Ct. Rev. 2002)

The only known appeal of a decision of the secret Foreign Intelligence Surveillance Court. It interpreted the Patriot Act as having lowered the standard the government must meet in order to conduct foreign intelligence surveillance.

Hirabayashi v. United States, 320 U.S. 81 (1943)

Held that the president had the power to impose a curfew on people of Japanese descent, including Japanese Americans, as an emergency wartime measure.

Korematsu v. United States, 323 U.S. 214 (1944)

Expanding on *Hirabayashi,* the Court held that people of Japanese descent could be excluded from certain areas of the United States. The effect of the exclusion order was their detention in internment camps.

Rasul v. Bush, 542 U.S. 466 (2004)

Concluded that federal habeas corpus statutes gave the Guantanamo detainees the right to challenge their detention in court. In response to *Rasul,* Congress passed new laws aimed at barring the courts from hearing detainees' petitions.

Youngstown Sheet & Tube Co. v. Sawyer, 343 U.S. 579, 634 (1952)
(Jackson, J., concurring)
Justice Robert Jackson's famous opinion that attempted to define the limits of presidential and congressional power.

Statutes

Public Law 107–40, Authorization for the Use of Military Force (AUMF) resolution
Passed nine days after the September 11 attacks, it authorized military force as retaliation against those responsible for the attacks and to prevent future acts of terrorism.

Public Law 107–56, the USA PATRIOT Act
Sweeping legislation that updated the federal criminal code and various other federal statutes to provide law enforcement agencies with additional legal tools to combat terrorism as well as ordinary crime.

Public Law 109–13, the REAL ID Act of 2005
Required states to meet stricter security measures with respect to driver's licenses and other identification documents.

Public Law 109–177, the USA PATRIOT Improvement and Reauthorization Act of 2005
(Actually signed into law in March 2006.) Re-enacted the original Patriot Act with only minor changes, and made most of its controversial provisions permanent.

Public Law 109–366, the Military Commissions Act of 2006
Drew up a set of rules governing military commission trials and incorporated them into the Uniform Code of Military Justice.

Public Law 110–53, the Implementing Recommendations of the 9/11 Commission Act of 2007
A wide-ranging measure aimed at carrying out many of the 9/11 Commission's recommendations.

Public Law 110–55, the Protect America Act of 2007
Amended the Foreign Intelligence Surveillance Act of 1978 to give the attorney general and the director of national intelligence wider discretion in monitoring telephone and e-mail communications to detect potential terrorist activity.

Terms and Concepts

9/11 Commission
acts of war
al Qaeda
Bush Doctrine

civil liberties
"clash of civilizations"
Combatant Status Review Tribunals
commander in chief power
data mining
due process of law
Foreign Intelligence Surveillance Act
Geneva Conventions
Guantanamo
habeas corpus
identity cards
International Criminal Court
international law
international terrorism
Iraq war
Islamism
jihad
law of armed conflict
Military Commissions Act
national security
neo-conservatism
Patriot Act
preemption
privacy
profiling
regime change
torture
unilateralism
unlawful combatant
War Powers Resolution
weapons of mass destruction

Introduction: September 11, Terrorism, and War

1 Daniel Benjamin and Steven Simon, *The Age of Sacred Terror* (New York,: Random House, 2002), 350–351.

2 United States Commission on National Security/21st Century, *New World Coming: American Security in the 21st Century* (Washington, D.C.: United States Commission on National Security/ 21st Century, 1999), 8.

3 National Commission on Terrorist Attacks Upon the United States, *The 9/11 Commission Report: Final Report of the National Commission on Terrorist Attacks Upon the United States* (New York: W.W. Norton & Company, 2004), 47.

4 *Ibid.*

5 Public Law 107–40.

6 George W. Bush, Address to Joint Session of Congress, September 20, 2001. Available online. URL: http://www.whitehouse .gov/news/releases/2001/09/20010920–8 .html. Accessed October 24, 2007.

7 *Ibid.*

8 Public Law 107–56.

9 George W. Bush, Graduation Speech, United States Military Academy, June 1, 2002. Available online. URL: http:// www.whitehouse.gov/news/releases/ 2002/06/20020601–3.html. Accessed October 24, 2007.

10 Office of the President of the United States, *The National Security Strategy of the United States of America* (Washington, D.C.: Office of the President of the United States, 2002), 6.

11 *Ibid.*, 23. (emphasis in the original)

Point: The United States Must Act Decisively to Defend Itself

1 George W. Bush, Remarks on Iraq, Cincinnati, Ohio, October 7, 2002. Available online. URL: http://www.whitehouse .gov/news/releases/2002/10/20021007–8 .html. Accessed October 24, 2007.

2 George W. Bush, State of the Union Address, January 29, 2002. Available online. URL: http://www.whitehouse .gov/news/releases/2002/01/20020129–11 .html. Accessed October 24, 2007.

3 Office of the President of the United States, *The National Security Strategy of the United States of America*, 18.

4 John F. Kennedy, Radio and Television Report to the American People on the Soviet Arms Buildup in Cuba, October 22, 1962. Available online. URL: http://www.jfklibrary.org. Accessed October 24, 2007.

5 Perle is quoted in Gary Schmitt, *Memorandum to Opinion Leaders: Richard Perle on Iraq* (Washington, D.C.: Project for the New American Century, 2003). Available online. URL: http:// www.newamericancentury.org/ iraq-20030224.htm. Accessed October 24, 2007.

6 George W. Bush, Remarks at Whitehall Palace, London, England, November 19, 2003. Available online. URL: http://www .whitehouse.gov/news/releases/2003/ 11/20031119–1.html. Accessed October 24, 2007.

7 Max Boot, *The Savage Wars of Peace: Small Wars and the Rise of American Power* (New York: Basic Books, 2002), 349.

8 Victor Davis Hanson, *An Autumn of War: What America Learned From September 11 and the War on Terrorism* (New York: Random House, 2002), 18.

9 Schmitt, *Memorandum to Opinion Leaders.*

10 Carla Anne Robbins, "Operation Bypass: Why the U.S. Gave the U.N. No Role in Plan to Halt Arms Ships," *Wall Street Journal*, October 21, 2003.

11 David B. Rivkin Jr. and Lee A. Casey, "The Rocky Shoals of International Law," *The National Interest* 62 (Winter 2000/2001): 35.

12 David Frum and Richard Perle, *An End to Evil: How to Win the War on Terror* (New York: Random House, 2003), 23.

13 Max Boot, "Surging Ahead in Iraq," *Wall Street Journal*, May 15, 2007.

Counterpoint: Unilateralism and Preemptive War Do More Harm Than Good

1 United Nations Security Council Resolution No. 1378 (November 14, 2001).

2 Jeffrey Record, *Bounding the Global War on Terrorism* (Carlisle, PA: U.S. Army War College, 2003), 49 (footnote 51).

3 Association of the Bar of New York City, Committee on International Security Affairs, *The Legality and Constitutionality of the President's*

Authority to Initiate an Invasion of Iraq. Draft (New York: Association of the Bar of New York City, 2002), 12. Available online. URL: http://www.abcny.org/pdf/report/Iraq2.pdf. Accessed October 24, 2007.

4 George W. Bush, State of the Union Address, January 28, 2003. Available online. URL: http://www.whitehouse.gov/news/releases/2003/01/20030128–19.html. Accessed October 24, 2007.

5 Joseph C. Wilson IV, "What I Didn't Find in Africa," *New York Times*, July 6, 2003.

6 Michael Ignatieff, "Why Are We in Iraq? (And Liberia? And Afghanistan?)," *New York Times Magazine*, September 7, 2003, 38.

7 Richard A. Falk, "The Aftermath of 9/11 and the Search for Limits: In Defense of Just War Thinking," ed. Charles W. Kegley, Jr., *The New Global Terrorism: Characteristics, Causes, Controls* (Upper Saddle River, N.J.: Prentice-Hall, 2003), 218.

8 George McGovern and William R. Polk, *Out of Iraq: A Practical Plan for With-drawal Now* (New York: Simon & Schuster, 2006), 131.

9 Michael Howard, "What's in a Name? How to Fight Terrorism," *Foreign Affairs* 81 no. 1 (January/February 2002): 8.

10 Geoffrey Perret, *Commander in Chief: How Truman, Johnson, and Bush Turned Presidential Power Into a Threat to America's Future* (New York: Farrar, Straus, and Giroux, 2007), 11.

11 James Fallows, "Declaring Victory," *The Atlantic*, September 2006, 60.

12 Michael Ignatieff, "Why America Must Know Its Limits," *Financial Times*, December 24, 2003.

13 *Ibid.*

14 *Ibid.*

Point: Military Justice Is an Appropriate Way to Deal with Terrorists

1 *Hamdi v. Rumsfeld*, 542 U.S. 507, 518–519 (2004).

2 *Hirabayashi* v. *United States*, 320 U.S. 81, 93 (1943).

3 *Hamdan v. Rumsfeld*, 548 U.S. —, —, 165 L.Ed.2d 723, 807 (2006) (Thomas, J., dissenting.).

4 David B. Rivkin Jr. and Lee A. Casey, "Guantanamo on Trial: The Red Cross Makes a Big Mistake in Siding With Detained Terrorists," *Wall Street Journal*, November 19, 2003.

5 Bradford A. Berenson, "Earth to Second Circuit: We're At War," *Wall Street Journal*, December 29, 2003.

6 National Commission on Terrorist Attacks Upon the United States, *The 9/11 Commission Report*, 72.

7 Berenson, "Earth to Second Circuit."

8 Professor Wedgwood is quoted in Kenneth Anderson, "What to Do with Bin Laden and Al Qaeda Terrorists?: A Qualified Defense of Military Commissions and United States Policy on Detainees at Guantanamo Bay Naval Base," *Harvard Journal of Law & Public Policy* 25(2), (Spring 2002): 593.

9 Bradford A. Berenson, "Terrorist Safe Haven," *Wall Street Journal*, June 14, 2007.

10 Michael B. Mukasey, "Jose Padilla Makes Bad Law," *Wall Street Journal*, August 22, 2007.

11 Public Law 109–366.

12 Robert H. Bork, "Civil Liberties After 9/11," *Commentary* 116, no. 29 (2003): 29.

Counterpoint: The War on Terror Violates Human Rights

1 William H. Rehnquist, *All Laws But One: Civil Liberties in Wartime* (New York: Alfred A. Knopf, 1998), 224–225.

2 Anne-Marie Slaughter, "Beware the Trumpets of War: A Response to Kenneth Anderson," *Harvard Journal of Law & Public Policy* 25, no. 2 (Summer 2002): 965.

3 Howard, "What's in a Name?," 8.

4 Diane F. Orentlicher and Robert K. Goldman, "When Justice Goes to War: Prosecuting Terrorists Before Military Commissions," *Harvard Journal of Law & Public Policy* 25, no. 2 (Summer 2002): 965.

5 Mark Denbeaux and Joshua Denbeaux, *Report on Guantanamo Detainees: A Profile of 517 Detainees Through Analysis of Department of Defense Data.* Interim Report (Newark, N.J.: Seton Hall University Law School, 2006).

Available online. URL: http://law.shu.
edu/news/guantanamo_reports.htm.
Accessed October 24, 2007.
6 Al Gore, "Freedom and Security," Address
to MoveOn.org, November 9, 2003.
Available online. URL: http://www
.truthout.org/docs_03/111103C.shtml.
Accessed October 24, 2007.
7 10 U.S.C. §948(1)(A).
8 *Ibid.*
9 American Bar Association Task Force on
Terrorism and the Law, *Report and Rec-
ommendation on Military Commissions*
(Chicago: American Bar Association,
2002), 6. Available online. URL: http://
www.abanet.org/leadership/military.pdf.
Accessed October 24, 2007.
10 Orentlicher and Goldman, "When Justice
Goes to War," 653.
11 Mark Denbeaux and Joshua Denbeaux,
*No-Hearing Hearings. CSRT: The Modern
Habeas Corpus? An Analysis of the Proceedings of the Government's Combatant
Status Review Tribunals at Guantanamo*
(Newark, N.J.: Seton Hall School of Law,
2006). Available online. URL: http://law
.shu.edu/news/guantanamo_reports
.htm. Accessed October 24, 2007.
12 Tim Golden, "For Guantanamo Review
Boards, Limits Abound," *New York
Times*, December 31, 2006.
13 John V. Whitbeck, " 'Terrorism': The
Word Itself is Dangerous," *Washington
Report on Middle East Affairs* 21 (March
2002): 52.
14 Gore, "Freedom and Security."
15 Edwin Dobb, "Should John Walker Lindh
Go Free?" *Harper's Magazine*, May 2002,
31.
16 *Hamdan v. Rumsfeld*, 548 U.S. —, —, 165
L.Ed.2d 723, 773 (2006).

**Point: New Laws Are Needed to
Fight Terrorism**
1 John Ashcroft, *Never Again: Securing
America and Restoring Justice* (New
York: Center Street, 2006), 286.
2 *Congressional Record*, October 25, 2001.
3 John Ashcroft, *Never Again*, 156.
4 Fitzgerald is quoted in John Ashcroft,
Never Again, 150.
5 National Commission on Terrorist Attacks
Upon the United States, *The 9/11 Commission Report*, 271.

6 John Ashcroft, *Never Again*, 158.
7 §215, Public Law 107–56, The USA
PATRIOT Act.
8 John Ashcroft, *Never Again*, 155.
9 Kim R. Holmes and Edwin Meese, III,
*The Administration's Anti-Terrorism
Package: Balancing Security and Liberty.*
Heritage Foundation Backgrounder
No. 1484. Washington, D.C.: Heritage Foundation, 2001, 3. Available
online. URL: http://www.heritage.org/
Research/HomelandSecurity/BG1486
.cfm. Accessed October 24, 2007.
10 *Ibid.*

**Counterpoint: Anti-terrorism Laws
Are Ineffective and Dangerous**
1 Public Law 110–55.
2 Whitbeck, " 'Terrorism,' " 52.
3 Center for Constitutional Rights, *The State
of Civil Liberties*, 10.
4 Eric Lichtblau, "U.S. Uses Terror Law to Pursue Crimes From Drugs to Swindling,"
New York Times, September 28, 2003.
5 *Ibid.*
6 Statement of Glenn A. Fine, Inspector
General, U.S. Department of Justice,
Before the House Permanent Select
Committee on Intelligence, March 28,
2007.
7 American Civil Liberties Union, Section
215 FAQ (New York: American Civil
Liberties Union, 2002). Available online.
URL: http://www.aclu.org/privacy/
spying/15423res20021024.html. Accessed
October 24, 2007.
8 *Center for National Security Studies* v.
Department of Justice, 331 F.3d 918, 947
(D.C. Cir. 2003) (Tatel, J., dissenting).
9 Ronald Dworkin, "Terror & the Attack
on Civil Liberties," *New York Review of
Books*, November 6, 2003, 17.
10 McGovern and Polk, *Out of Iraq*, 126.
11 U.S. Department of Transportation, *Traffic Safety Facts* (Washington, D.C.: 2001).
Available online. URL: http://www-nrd
.nhtsa.dot.gov/pdf/nrd-30/NCSA/
TSFAnn/TSF2001.pdf. Accessed October 24, 2007.
12 John Mueller, *Overblown: How Politicians and the Terrorism Industry Inflate
National Security Threats and Why We
Believe Them* (New York: Free Press,
2006), 29.

13 Mueller, *Overblown*, 193.

14 Senator Russ Feingold, "On Opposing the U.S.A. Patriot Act," Address to the Associated Press Managing Editors Conference, Milwaukee, Wisconsin, October 12, 2001. Available online. URL: http://www .archipelago.org/vol6–2/feingold.htm. Accessed October 24, 2007.

15 *Ibid.*

16 Professor Cole is quoted in Gregg Krupa and John Bebow, "Immigration Crackdown Snares Arabs," *Detroit News*, November 3, 2003.

17 Gore, "Freedom and Security."

Conclusion: The Future of the War on Terror

1 Office of the President, *National Security Strategy 2002*, 31.

2 Frum and Perle, *An End to Evil: How to Win the War on Terror*, 70.

3 Michael Smerconish, *Flying Blind: How Political Correctness Continues to Compromise Airline Safety Post 9/11* (Philadelphia: Running Press, 2004), 12.

4 Bob Barr, "Patriot Act Games: It Can Happen Here," *The American Spectator*, August/September 2003, 34.

5 Samuel P. Huntington, "The Clash of Civilizations," *Foreign Affairs* 72, no. 3 (1993), 22.

6 Editorial, "W Ducks Real Nature of War U.S. Is In," *New York Daily News*, October 29, 2003.

7 National Intelligence Council, *National Intelligence Estimate: The Terrorist Threat to the US Homeland* (Washington, D.C., 2007). Available online. URL: http://www.dni.gov/press_releases/ 20070717_release.pdf. Accessed October 24, 2007.

8 Jeanne Meserve, "Sources: Staged Cyber Attack Reveals Vulnerability in Power Grid," CNN.com, September 26, 2007.

9 National Intelligence Council, *National Intelligence Estimate.*

10 David Rohde, "Radical Islam Gains a Seductive New Voice," *New York Times*, October 26, 2003.

11 George W. Bush, Address to Joint Session of Congress, September 20, 2001.

12 James Fallows, "Declaring Victory."

13 Hanson, *An Autumn of War: What America Learned From September 11 and the War on Terrorism*, 76.

14 Daniel Benjamin and Steven Simon, *The Next Attack: The Failure of the War on Terror and a Strategy for Getting It Right* (New York: Henry Holt, 2005), 126.

15 Benjamin and Simon, *The Age of Sacred Terror*, 411.

16 *Ibid.*, 419.

RESOURCES /////▷

Books

Ashcroft, John. *Never Again: Securing America and Restoring Justice*. New York: Center Street, 2006.

Benjamin, Daniel, and Steven Simon. *The Next Attack: The Failure of the War on Terror and a Strategy for Getting It Right*. New York: Henry Holt, 2005.

Boot, Max. *The Savage Wars of Peace: Small Wars and the Rise of American Power*. New York: Basic Books, 2002.

Frum, David, and Richard Perle. *An End to Evil: How to Win the War on Terror*. New York: Random House, 2003.

Mueller, John. *Overblown: How Politicians and the Terrorism Industry Inflate National Security Threats and Why We Believe Them*. New York: Free Press, 2006.

Rehnquist, William H. *All Laws But One: Civil Liberties in Wartime*. New York: Alfred A. Knopf, 1998.

Reports

National Commission on Terrorist Attacks Upon the United States. *The 9/11 Commission Report: Final Report of the National Commission on Terrorist Attacks Upon the United States*. New York: W.W. Norton & Company, 2004.

Office of the President of the United States. *The National Security Strategy of the United States of America*. Washington, D.C.: Office of the President of the United States, 2006.

Record, Jeffrey. *Bounding the Global War on Terrorism*. Carlisle, Penn.: U.S. Army War College, 2003.

Web Sites

American Civil Liberties Union
http://www.aclu.org
> The nation's oldest and best-known civil liberties organization. The ACLU has gone to court on a number of occasions to challenge anti-terrorism laws.

Brookings Institute
http://www.brookings.org
> An independent research and advocacy organization. Some of its scholars have been critical of Bush administration policies.

142

Center for Constitutional Rights

http://www.ccr-ny.org

A legal and educational organization dedicated to protecting rights guaranteed by the Bill of Rights and the Universal Declaration of Human Rights.

Department of State

http://www.state.gov

The Executive Branch department that is responsible for foreign policy.

Electronic Frontier Foundation

http://eff.org

An organization that argues for online privacy and civil liberties. EFF is especially critical of government surveillance of citizens' communications.

Electronic Privacy Information Center

http://www.epic.org

An advocacy organization that opposed the Patriot Act and objects to the government's efforts to gather more information about Americans.

Heritage Foundation

http://www.heritage.org

A conservative research and advocacy organization that supports the Bush Doctrine, the Patriot Act, and aggressive measures to fight terrorists.

Human Rights First

http://www.humanrightsfirst.org

An organization whose mission is to protect "people at risk," including victims of human rights abuses.

MoveOn.org

http://www.moveon.org

A liberal, Internet-based organization that opposes Bush administration policies, especially the Iraq war.

Preserving Life & Liberty

http://www.lifeandliberty.gov

A Web site established by the U.S. Justice Department to make the case for anti-terrorism legislation, especially the Patriot Act.

Project for a New American Century

http://www.newamericancentury.org

The leading neo-conservative advocacy organization. Neo-conservatives believe that the United States should remain the world's preeminent nation and should use its power—including military force—to stop other countries' governments from oppressing their people, threatening their neighbors, or aiding terrorists.

The Weekly Standard

http://www.weeklystandard.com

An influential magazine that supports neo-conservative policies.

The White House

http://www.whitehouse.gov

The official Web site of the president and vice president of the United States. It contains an archive of presidential addresses.

PAGE

INDEX

CONTRIBUTORS ||||▷

PAUL RUSCHMANN, J.D., is a legal analyst and writer based in Canton, Michigan. He received his undergraduate degree from the University of Notre Dame and his law degree from the University of Michigan. He is a member of the State Bar of Michigan. His areas of specialization include legislation, public safety, traffic and transportation, and trade regulation. He is also the author of nine other books in the POINT/COUNTERPOINT series, which deal with such issues as the military draft, indecency in the media, and private property rights, and is the author of the first edition of *War on Terror*. He can be found online at *www.PaulRuschmann.com*.

ALAN MARZILLI, M.A., J.D., lives in Birmingham, Alabama, and is a program associate with Advocates for Human Potential, Inc., a research and consulting firm based in Sudbury, Mass., and Albany, N.Y. He primarily works on developing training and educational materials for agencies of the federal government on topics such as housing, mental health policy, employment, and transportation. He has spoken on mental health issues in 30 states, the District of Columbia, and Puerto Rico; his work has included training mental health administrators, nonprofit management and staff, and people with mental illnesses and their families on a wide variety of topics, including effective advocacy, community-based mental health services, and housing. Marzilli has written several handbooks and training curricula that are used nationally and as far away as the U.S. territory of Guam. Additionally, he managed statewide and national mental health advocacy programs and worked for several public interest lobbying organizations while studying law at Georgetown University. Marzilli has written more than a dozen books, including numerous titles in the POINT/COUNTERPOINT series.